Music Talks

Roberto Cruciani

1 - The Intervals

Art cover:
Walking the bass
Analog collage by Elsa Botting Leone
Instagram: elsabottingleone

To contact the author:
robcrucianibass@gmail.com

ISBN: 9798802330241
Independently published

Table of contents

Foreword

Have you ever wondered how a certain song can stir an emotion deep inside of you? How can it evoke a specific mood? How can it awaken a memory inside you, or a sensation that you might never have even experienced personally?

This book tries to delve into these questions. This is the first of a series of three books dedicated to the analysis of the founding principles of the music that surrounds us everyday. Two more books will follow this: *From Intervals to Melody* and *Musical Structures*. Though they deal with rather technical and specific topics, these texts are addressed to anyone who has enough passion about music to be willing to investigate its mysteries: from musicians to theorists, from music critics to simple enthusiasts. These books are not devised to give notions, rather, they aim at providing tools to understand the basic mechanisms of musical competence, for the musician as well as for the listener. An investigation on how composers' and musicians' choices relate to the innate or learned structures we use as music listeners in our historical and cultural context. In order to carry out these investigations, I will rely on my academic studies in semiology of music, ethnomusicology, harmony and counterpoint, musical anthropology and on my personal experience as a musician and as an insatiable music listener.

In this book we will deal with the founding element that is at the very base of any musical experience: the interval. We will isolate it, in order to highlight its more distinguishing aspects, associated with its semantic field in our historical and cultural context. All the intervals will be examined, one after the other, with a series of examples drawn from worldwide known songs, from different times and genres, as much as possible. I am a rock bass player, specialised in blues and psychedelic music. Therefore, many examples will come from this background. By choosing these examples, I hope to create interest in those who already know the songs but rarely find them in music theory books, and also in those who don't know them but will be curious enough to listen to them and discover them.

When writing a book like this, many mistakes occur: I know this from experience. I already know that I will probably find these texts naïve and inaccurate when I read them in a couple of years. So I ask the attentive reader, who might find these inaccuracies already on his first reading, to be benevolent and look instead at the general picture and at the proposed approach to understand the basic mechanisms for creating and listening to music.

I am confident that at the end of this journey the reader will gain a set of tools for the analysis of music. It may be that he could also be able to use them as a springboard to dive into experimentations and take these mechanisms beyond the scopes proposed in this book. Or it may be that some musicologist with a better understanding of some aspects will be stirred to share his own perspective to enrich everyone's musical experience.

The books in this series isolate some aspects or concepts, which I consider essential, in the attempt to observe them under the microscope, and bring to light elements otherwise hidden in the background. I feel it is very important, though, to stress that any musical analysis can not be grounded on isolated details of the musical experience. It should instead try and integrate all the pieces of knowledge provided in these books and maybe other specific knowledge as well.

I believe that a better musical awareness and a sharper musical knowledge are important tools for the human being as a musical being in a musical world. We are all surrounded by sounds and music, from those in supermarkets to the radio in our cars, from movies to advertisements, from announcements at the airport or at the station to the music on hold on the phone. What we usually underestimate is the accuracy of the choice of all this music and of all these sounds. It doesn't matter if there is a deceiving mind behind these choices, or if there is a simple awareness of musical competence. What really matters is that, if we are not able to recognise them and maybe value them, we end up being passive receivers. In some ways, musical competence is innate, while in some other ways it is a cultural acquisition. Being aware of your own cultural or innate abilities is both a personal and social growth in any case.

Chapter 1
The basic concepts

Take a string, for example, a guitar string. Make it vibrate. The sound you hear is measurable as frequency, that is, we can create a graphic representation of it as a wave. This wave moves over and below an imaginary line cutting the wave in the middle of its amplitude: the number of times this wave crosses the line within a second is what we call frequency. The higher the pitch, the higher the frequency. On the other hand, the lower the pitch, the lower the frequency: 1 Hertz means just one crossing in a second. As per convention, the 'central *A*' note corresponds with 440Hz. Now press the string at half its length, so that only half of the string is vibrating. Hint: on a guitar this corresponds to the twelfth fret. The sound you get now when the string vibrates corresponds to double the frequency of the previous sound. In the case of the *A* string, now we have a vibration of 880Hz. The distance between these two notes, the relation between them, is an interval of one *octave*. You will notice that our ear perceives these two sounds as the same note at a different pitch. In fact, if we look at them from the perspective of the physics of sound, these two notes share the same harmonics, that is the several less intense 'overtones' that make up the basic sound. In musical anthropology, this feeling of the octave as the same note is known as an 'absolute' feature, that is something we can find in every culture, as opposed to elements, like scales, which are defined as 'cultural' features, because they change according to place and time. To us, this means we can limit our definition of intervals within the range of the octave, since the same scheme will repeat at a different pitch.

Musical intervals indicate the relationship between two notes. They measure the distance between two notes, the space between them. We can figure out this space literally, for example visualising it as the distance between two keys on a piano keyboard, or between two frets on a string instrument, like a guitar or a bass guitar.

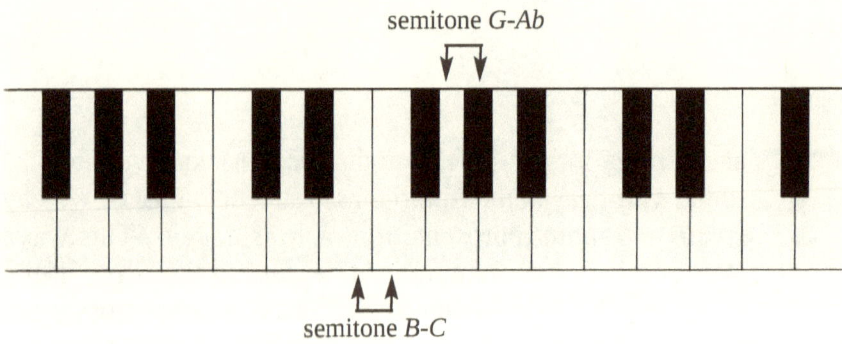

Fig. 1. Semitones on a keyboard and on a bass guitar.

Or we can think of it as the (vertical) space between two notes written on a music staff.

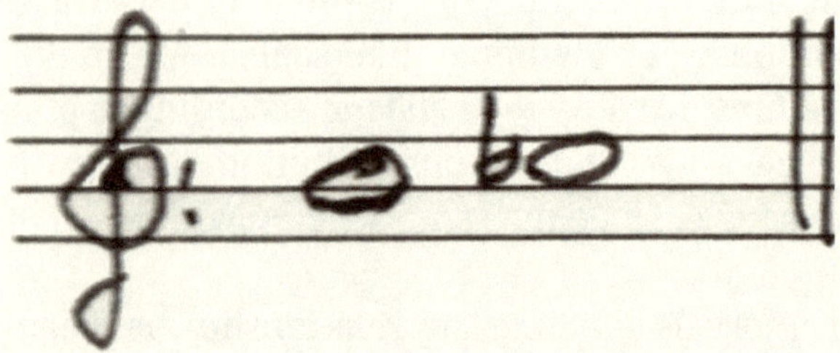

Fig. 2. The semitone G-Ab written on a music staff with a G-clef.

In all these cases, we have an accurate visual representation of the musical concept. You can think of intervals in whichever works best for you, however, it is useful to think of them as something concrete and not only conceptual.

Typologies of intervals

Intervals are the building blocks of music. They are the fundamental and guaranteed element in building melodies, chords, scales and anything that forms a part of music. If it is true that music is fundamentally made of relations, just as any other form of art, then we can claim that intervals are the essence of relation in music. But we need at least two sounds, two notes to create a relation, therefore an interval. It is easy to see how important the intervals are: take any simple melody and try to substitute a single note with any other note. You will get a completely different result, since the relation between the notes also defines and conveys a 'semantic field', allowing the music to convey a meaning, a mood, an emotion. Let's take *Space Oddity* by David Bowie: the sad and gloomy descending major second at the beginning of its melody immediately shows us the tragedy described in the lyrics, long before the lyrics tell us anything sad: "Ground control to major Tom". If we change that single interval in the melody, the whole sense we perceive of the song will change as well!

In the next chapters, we will analyze in depth every single interval within the range of the octave. And in the next book I will delve deeper into the analysis of the semantic fields connected to the intervals in the broader context of melody. For now let's get back to basics and try to define intervals and the terms used in music to identify them.

An interval can be made of two notes played at the same time: in this case, we will call it a *vertical interval* or *harmonic interval*. Vertical, since these two sounds occur at the same time and are written on staff one above the other. Harmonic, since the foundation of chords and of harmony is shown by two notes played simultaneously.

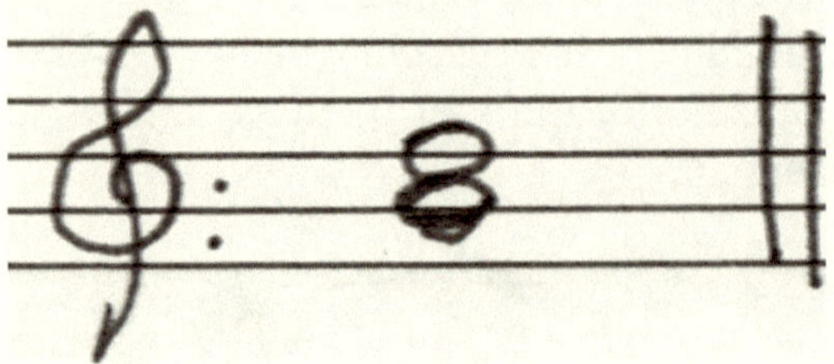

Fig. 3. Vertical or harmonic interval on a music staff. In this case, we see an interval of a major third made of the notes G and B, which are written one above the other to show that they are to be played simultaneously.

Or, the two notes of the interval can occur in a sequence, one after the other: in this case we call it *horizontal* or *melodic interval*. Horizontal, since the two notes are written on the staff following an imaginary line from left to right. The space between them will be measured through the time gap between the first and the second note. Melodic, since this is exactly the way we build a melody, or a scale: by creating a sequence of notes.

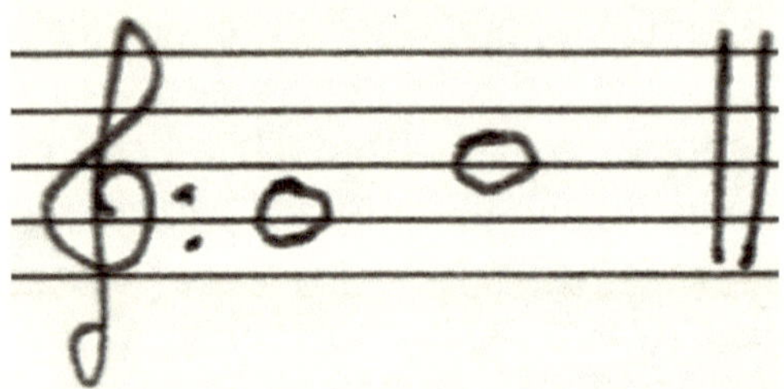

Fig. 4. Horizontal or melodic interval. Here we see the same notes of the previous example G and B, but the way they are written shows that they are to be played in sequence, not simultaneously.

If we visualize the interval as notes on a music staff, we clearly find the vertical and horizontal dimensions of these two types of intervals, as shown in the pictures.

We also distinguish intervals by looking at their direction. When the first note of our measurement is lower, deeper than the second

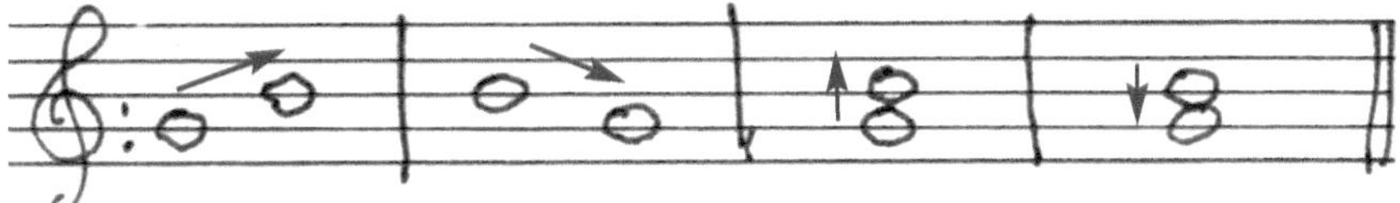

Fig. 5. Ascending and descending harmonic and melodic intervals.

note, then we will have an *ascending interval*. On the contrary, when the first note is higher than the second note, the interval will be *descending*. These distinctions appear to be quite intuitive in the case of a melodic interval. In fact, in music practice this directional distinction is almost exclusively used for melodic intervals. Theorically, though, also a harmonic interval can be ascending or descending, depending on which of the notes we take as the first note of our measurement. Usually we tend to start from the bottom when we measure harmonic intervals, therefore creating only ascending intervals. The direction of intervals is very important in creating the musical sense one wants to convey as well. There seems to be a correspondance between the perception of a descending interval and a physical descending movement, and vice versa, between an ascending interval and a physical ascending movement. This is another 'universal' phenomenon, in the anthropological sense. We can easily see this in dance movements. This correspondence, though, extends further, leading us to associate a descending movement with the idea of defeat, resignation, sadness, even death and burial, and at the same time nostalgia, cherished memory... The ascending movement is usually associated with the ideas of ascent, assertion, victory, triumph, and also joy, jumping... Again, we will look at this subject in depth further on in this book. For a deeper discussion of some particular intervals, please refer to the second book of this series *From Intervals to Melody*.

Measurement of intervals

In the meantime, let's go on with our definition of intervals and with our analysis of the related terms. If we want to define the distance between two sounds, we need a unit of measurement. In our

Western system based on the 'equal temperament', the shortest distance between two notes is the semitone. On a guitar or bass guitar it corresponds to the movement from one fret to the next, forward or backward; on a piano keyboard it corresponds to the distance between a key and the next, forward or backward (both white and black). The equal temperament is based on the subdivision of the interval of one octave in twelve equal parts, that is twelve semitones. Why do we call this interval an 'octave'? Because in our system scales are usually made of seven notes. The eighth note is the same as the first one at a different pitch. So it takes the role of the end of the sequence and, at the same time, of the beginning of a new identical sequence, where it is the starting note. In other words, we have names for seven notes: *A, B, C, D, E, F, G*. But not all the notes are separated by a tone from each other, since the intervals *B-C* and *E-F* cover a distance of just one semitone. In order to give names to the remaining notes on the other five semitones, we use alterations: sharp (#) to raise the note by a semitone (for example *C#*) and flat (*b*) to lower it by a semitone (for example *Db*).

In this way, we find ourselves with two names for some of the notes, which occupy the same place on an instrument and in fact sound perfectly identical, that is, they share the same frequency. These notes are called *enharmonic equivalents*. It is exactly the case of our example of *C#* and *Db*: they are indeed the same note, with a different name according to the context. Every scale is a sequence of intervals of semitone and tone (that is two semitones) and is built using the name of the seven notes. Therefore, if we start a major scale (or a minor scale) from *B*, the second note of the scale will necessarily be a *C*. The first interval of that scale, though, is a tone,

Fig. 6. The C major scale is made of only natural notes, without alterations, with the sequence T-T-S-T-T-T-S. If we start the scale from E, keeping the same sequence of Tones and Semitones, we need to raise F, G, C and D, which will become F#, G#, C# and D#. If we instead start the scale from F, we need to lower B to Bb.

while there is only a semitone between *B* and *C*. So we need to raise the *C* to *C#*, in order to get the interval of tone that we need. We won't call that note *Db*, because in the sequence of notes we have not used the *C*. In the same way, in a *G minor* scale, the sequence of intervals starts with Tone-Semitone. Therefore: *G, A, Bb*. We won't call the third note *A#*, even if it sounds the same, because we already used *A* for the second note.

So, using the semitone as a unit of measurement, let's see the names given to each interval. The first interval we can build is made with the repetition of the same note. Obviously, it is easier to imagine this as a melodic interval rather than a harmonic one. This interval is called *unison* (e.g. *C-C*). A semitone further on, we find the *interval of minor second* (e.g. *C-Db*). Two semitones away from our starting note we have the *major second* (e.g. *C-D*). The reason why we call both these intervals a 'second' is that in both cases we are using the second note from the starting one. For example, if we start from *C*, the 'second' note is *D*, to be precise *Db* if the distance is one semitone (minor second), or *D* if the distance is one tone (major second). Any interval wider than a tone in a sequence of notes does not satisfy the requirement of the scale for a sequence of tones and semitones. Therefore, when the distance between the notes measures one tone and a half (or three semitones), we call this interval *minor third* (*C-Eb*), while a *major third* (*C-E*) measures a distance of two tones (or four semitones).

For the intervals of fourth and fifth we need to delve into a different topic. They are both called *perfect*. The reason why they have this different classification lies in the concepts of *consonance* and *dissonance* and in the changes these concepts underwent throughout history. The most used compositive principle in ancient times, before the 18th century, was the *counterpoint*. Before being written on staff as we know today, notes were written as dots, *punctum* in Latin (plural: *puncta*). When two or more voices sang together, different notes occured at the same time, just as in our chords. The composers aimed at creating a melodic movement with several voices, taking into account these moments when the notes met, *puncta contra puncta*: this is the origin of the term 'counterpoint'. Some notes share many harmonics and therefore they sound pleasant together, conveying a sense of resolution: these are *consonant* combinations. Other notes share just a few harmonics, and so they create tension when played together: these are called *dissonant*. A calculated alternance of dissonances and consonances is the main requirement for a good musical piece. What is considered to be dissonant in a certain time, though, might be perceived as consonant in a different time. Partly, this comes also from the use, before the 18th century, of mathematical systems of subdivision of the octave that were different from the one we use today. Sometimes more than one system could be used at the same time. Usually, these systems are generically termed as pytagorean systems. In this context, for example, the position of the thirds could vary, slightly adjusting to the musical context. Therefore, it was not easy to consider them as consonant: while sometimes they were felt to be pleasant and resolved, as soon as the context slightly changed they were perceived as dissonant, producing tension. The only notes that were quite stable corresponded to the ones we find on the intervals of fourth and fifth (besides, obviously, the octave). That's why these intervals are still termed as 'perfect' instead of 'major' or 'minor'. And that's why they were considered as consonant. Nowadays, we build chords using thirds, which are consonant to our ears. But it is clear that the concepts of consonance and dissonance are extremely variable, not only from culture to culture, but also within the same culture in different times. Nonetheless, the names of the intervals remained the same.

So, an interval of two tones and a half (that is, five semitones) is called *perfect fourth* (*C-F*). If we add a semitone (three tones, that is six semitones) we get an *augmented fourth* (*C-F#*). Perfect intervals change in augmented when we add a semitone, diminished when we subtract a semitone. This interval at a distance of six semitones from the starting note is very peculiar, since it is placed exactly half way in the journey towards the octave (twelve semitones). Moreover, according to the situation, it can also be called *diminished fifth* (*C-Gb*). In fact, most musicians will preferably call it this way. This correspondence of two different intervals is another instance of enharmony, just like the two names of notes that indicate the same sound.

At a distance of three tones and a half (seven semitones), we find the *perfect fifth* (*C-G*), while at a distance of four tones (eight semitones) we get the *augmented fifth* (*C-G#*). Again, this is another instance of enharmony, since the same interval of eight semitones is often called a *minor sixth* (*C-Ab*).

The decision to use one definition or the other depends on the context. The same two sounds, for example, might occur within different scales. If the scales already have a note on the perfect fifth, we will choose to call our interval a minor sixth. If the sound corresponds to the fifth note of the scale, then we will call it an augmented fifth. We should also take into account some harmonic issues, related to the construction and to the function of the chords in the context we are analysing. In this book, we will use the most common definitions of the intervals: diminished fifth for the interval made of three tones, and minor sixth for the interval made of four tones. At a distance of four tones and a half from the starting note (nine semitones), we find the *major sixth* (*C-A*). Five tones away from our first note (ten semitones), we get the *minor seventh* (*C-Bb*). The last interval is the *major seventh* (*C-B*), five tones and a half (eleven semitones) from the starting note, followed only by the *octave* (*C-C*), six tones (or twelve semitones) away from the starting note. As we have already seen, the octave is also the starting note for a new set of intervals at a higher pitch.

Inversions

Finally, a very important concept about intervals that is often confusing: we'd better make it clear before going deeper in the analysis of the specific intervals. I'm talking about the *inversions* of the intervals. The relationships between two notes, for example *C* and *E*, depends on many factors. We already saw the difference between a harmonic interval and a melodic interval: the effect is not totally different, in the end it is the same interval, and yet our ear perceives the relationship between the notes in a slightly different way. In addition, we need to consider the *direction* of the interval: if *C* is the lower note of the couple, we get an *ascending major third*. If we change the direction of the interval, considering the higher note as our starting point, we get a *descending major third, E-C*, with rather different features. I challenge you to test these intervals, by first playing a melodic interval *C-E* and then an interval *E-C*. They are the same notes, therefore these intervals share many features, and yet our ear perceives them as different relationships. When we talk of interval *inversions*, what we do is keep the same two notes and *the same direction*, moving one of the notes to a different octave: *C* to the higher octave, or *E* to the lower octave. In this way, the *ascending interval C-E* becomes the *ascending interval E-C*, an *ascending minor sixth*. In a certain sense, the inversion is a mirror image of the original interval. Inversions can also occur within chords, by moving one or more chord tones to a higher or lower octave, creating *chord inversions*. The basic chords are made of three notes and are called triads: therefore it is possible to build two inversions. The first inversion moves the first chord tone, the lower note, to the next higher octave. The second inversion moves both the first and the second chord tone to the next higher octave.

Fig. 7. The basic triad of the E minor chord and its inversions, built by moving the lower note to the next higher octave.

If we want to quickly discover what interval comes from the inversion of another interval, we can use what I call the 'rule of nine': adding an interval and its inversion we always get nine, not eight. For example, the inversion of a second is always a seventh (2+7=9), the inversion of a third is always a sixth (3+6=9) and so on. Moreover, a major interval will always invert in a minor interval and vice versa: the inversion of major second (*C-D*) is a minor seventh (*D-C*), the inversion of a minor third (*A-C*) is always a major sixth (*C-A*). Inversions of perfect intervals remain perfect: the inversion of a perfect fourth (*C-F*) is a perfect fifth (*F-C*), the inversion of a perfect fifth (*C-G*) is a perfect fourth (*G-C*). The dimininshed fifth is exaclty halfway in the octave. Therefore, its inversion will remain the same, a diminished fifth (*F-B, B-F*). Though in this case it would be more precise to call it an augmented fourth.

Intervals and ear training

An interval is the interaction or the relation between two notes. But I believe that the place where this interaction occurs is the listener's ear. I strongly believe that all the semantic fields associated with the intervals are not an embedded feature of the intervals themselves, but rather that they depend on the interpretation that the listener gives them. In this sense, we could claim that the musician is a sort of 'first listener', who applies himself to test the effectiveness of the notes he makes use of, and who plays with the expectations of the listener's ear and interpretation. Let me start by saying that here we are not looking for inviolable rules and features; we are looking for the mechanisms that fill the musical communicative act with sense, in the space between the musician, the sounds and the listener. Therefore, the ear is the most important instrument for any musician.

A minority of people have the so-called absolute pitch. This means that they can identify the pitch of a note without the help of any reference to rely on. Without a doubt, it is a gift, for those who choose to be musicians. Although, it can become a drawback. Imagine how annoying it must be to listen to sounds that are out of tune especially in the context of a concert! And what about the ancient tunings? In Verdi's time, it was a common practice in France to tune the central *A* at 435Hz. Verdi himself fostered the standardization of tuning in Italy, with the central *A* at 432Hz, basing his proposal on Sauveur's so-called 'scientific tuning', which placed its reference on a *C* at 256Hz. Recently, this battle involving the shift in tuning of the central *A* at 432Hz started again, with a series of famous musical pieces based on this reference (for example by Pink Floyd). What a nightmare the uncertainty of intonation must be for someone who has a perfect pitch! Apparently, perfect pitch often goes along with a certain form of synesthesia, where colours are associated with sounds. Synesthesia is a sensorial-perceptive phenomenon that involves several senses at the same time, senses that are not usually involved in the perception of a given stimulus. Many disadvantages seem to come from this phenomenon as well. Musicologist Adam

Neely, in a pedagogical video on Youtube, claimed to have a certain degree of synesthesia, since he sees and associates colours to the sounds he perceives. He apologised to any of his viewers with the same condition, so that the way it is represented in the video might not be accurate for everybody!

Ear training is a pedagogical practice that aims instead at developing a *relative ear*, namely the trained ability to identify the interaction between notes, rather than identifying absolute frequencies. It is an extremely useful ability for any musician who does not have absolute pitch. And it is also a practice that can be really helpful for those who have absolute pitch, in order to overcome its disadvantages. Obviously, dealing with the interaction between notes, it is mainly based on identifying intervals: harmonic intervals, melodic intervals, ascending intervals, descending intervals and inversions. Then it goes on to the identification of chords made of at least three notes and of the functional relationships between chords in a harmonic sequence. It is possible to train the relative ear by having someone play some notes on an instrument and by trying to guess the interval or the chord, without looking at the instrument. By using this method, you start 'blindly' until you build some reference from which to move on. It might sound strange, but this learning method brings some advantages. Anthropologist Gregory Bateson, in *Angels Fear: Towards an Epistemology of the Sacred* (Macmillan, 1987), calls it the skeet shooting learning method, opposed to the archery learning method. In archery, you don't shoot the arrow until you are certain of the target. Every shot is an isolated journey, independent from the previous one, apart from the complete inner awareness of breathing, of the physical posture and so on. All the process is an 'inner' job, so to speak, and it only secondarily deals with the shooting and with the target. In skeet shooting, on the other hand, there is no other way than to go by trial and error, adjusting the aim on previous errors. If you look at it this way, the blind method already seems to be more serious, doesn't it? Nowadays there are several apps for smartphones that allow us to train our ear almost like playing a game. The downside, obviously, is that sounds from a smartphone are less rich than those generated by an instrument. The upside is that the blind method is organised, limiting the choices at our disposal: for example we could start with the challenge of identifying two similar intervals, say a minor third and a major third, developing our discerning abilities step by step. Another very useful technique for interval recognition consists in creating your own mental repertoire of melodies or musical phrases, each one featuring one of the intervals. A melody for the unison, one for the ascending minor second, one for the descending minor second and so on. You need to choose melodies or musical phrases that you know very well, so that you can recall them at any time to get a reference by which you can confront the unknown interval you want to define. It takes a very long time to find melodies or musical phrases for each one of the possible intervals, but it is worth it.

This kind of work is strictly connected with what Edwin Gordon defined 'audiation' in 1986, playing with the similarity of the word 'imagination': essentially, the ability of imagining sounds. On this concept, Gordon grounded his Music Learning Theory, that was really revolutionary for his time. According to Gordon, "audiation is to music what thought is to speech". Audiation 'occurs' when someone is "listening to, recalling, performing, interpreting, creating, improvising, reading or writing music". Any experienced musician knows this phenomenon as a personal experience, just like when a simple sound, for example a squeaking door, stirs our imagination or memory of a melody, a song or even a single musical element. We might say that ear training is a method to train this inborn ability of every human being.

Intervals and musical context

To conclude this chapter on the definitions of intervals, I would like to stress an aspect that is often underrated. Usually, we tend to consider intervals in isolation from the context. This might seem an aseptic and scientific approach, but it doesn't always pay off in practical terms. It is a good starting point, whereas isolating the elements we are learning about helps us set up limits and focus on our efforts. But at a certain point, we will need to put the intervals in their context. For example, an interval *E-F* is without a doubt an ascending minor second, but it can present different nuances if the tonal reference is *F* or *C*, if it is a movement from the seventh note of the scale to the eighth (or first), or if it is a movement from the third note to the fourth note of the scale. The differences might be very subtle, but it is right in the smallest details that every musician builds his own technique.

On the other hand, there's a much more evident aspect related to the semantic fields and the melodic movements. It is true that every interval builds a certain semantic field, but it is also necessary to consider the whole melodic movement of which the interval is part. A melodic phrase is a sequence of notes ending with a full stop, both in rhythm and harmony. It might be a sequence framed between two pauses. It might be an arch, or a more or less straight line, reaching a resolving point after a moment of tension. And all this can occur using bigger or smaller ranges between the lower note and the higher note of the whole melodic movement. Even when these two notes are not close to each other, the interaction between them might be very important in conveying the sense of the whole melodic phrase and in tingeing the sense of the intervals within it. This interval is what we call melodic range.

Again, for a deeper discussion of this topic, please refer to the book *From Intervals to Melody*.

Chapter 2
The unison

Harmonic interval

The unison is the interval generated by two identical notes, even at the same pitch. We could call it interval zero, since the distance between the notes equals zero. Consequently, it is not easy to imagine situations where this interval occurs as a vertical, harmonic interval. It is impossible to perform it on a single musical instrument, or a single voice. Therefore, the only remaining cases are those where these two identical notes are simultaneously performed by different instruments or voices. In general, it has the effect of reinforcing, specifically of increasing the volume of the sound played. An orchestra's section comes to mind, where several musicians play the same notes in unison, to create a louder sound. In this case, it is interesting to note the slight, almost imperceptible shift in the performance of the musicians. This is something more and more difficult to value in a world made of synthetic sounds and quantizing... I also think of *Hoochie Coochie Man*'s first recording – the famous blues by Willie Dixon recorded by Muddy Waters in 1954 (with Willie Dixon himself on bass). The song's distinguishing riff, a milestone in modern history of music, is performed by the instruments in unison. But what makes that recording so beautiful is exactly the fact that there's a very slight shift between the instruments. Many more recent versions, recorded by so many bluesmen, gave up this element, opting for a better precision. I think some of the beauty of that riff got lost in this way. To be precise, this is not a proper unison, since bass and guitar, for example, perform the riff on different octaves. On the other hand, we already know the tight relationship that connects the unison and the octave, that will be discussed further on in

Fig. 8. Hoochie Coochie Man's *riff.*

this book. Anyway, among the instruments playing the riff, there are also a harp and a piano. This slight shift in the performance of the different instruments enhances the difference in the various instruments' timbre, which maybe is the most interesting effect a harmonic unison can produce.

Melodic interval

As a horizontal, melodic interval, the unison obviously is easier to find and can present several nuances. In general, we can think of it as a stop, a waiting, a sense of monotony, but also as the preparation for a jump... A simple melody like *Jingle Bells* (James Lord Pierpont, 1857) is strongly connoted by the repetition of its first note, in two separate melodic figures, before the wider melodic jump ("Jingle all the way"), that results even more satisfying and incisive after all this stagnation. A very similar case is *Happy Birthday to You* (Mildred Hill, 1893), where the word "birthday" is highlighted by its preparation with a repeated note on the previous two syllables on "happy".

Fig. 9. Jingle Bells

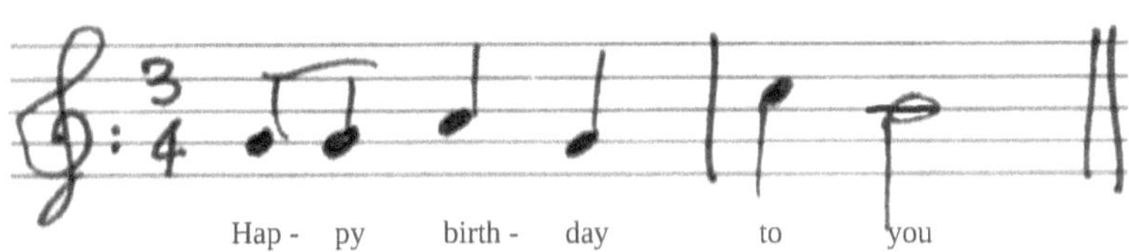

Fig. 10. Happy Birthday to You

The main difference between these two examples is that the unison in *Jingle Bells* is followed by an ascending jump which is quite wide, while in *Happy Birthday to You* the following interval is small (a major second) and goes back to the tonic note before ending the musical phrase. Therefore, we can say that the movement and the size of the following or preceding intervals have a great impact on the unison.

There are an endless number of examples of melodies starting with a repeated note. Among these, just think of The Beatles' *Let It Be* or *Michelle*, also by The Beatles. In *Let It Be*, we find a tighter rhythm, with the melody proceeding to a wavy evolution with a quite long arch, before the melodic phrase's conclusion ("When I find myself in times of trouble"). On the other hand, in *Michelle* the two repeated notes are long notes, followed by a wider interval, that takes the melody even lower than the starting note. The first sentence ends rather soon ("Michelle, ma belle"), like a sort of determined claim.

Fig. 11. The Beatles, Let It be.

Fig. 12. The Beatles, Michelle.

Fig. 13. Elton John, Candle in the Wind.

Or maybe like the beginning of a letter. This effect is in many ways similar to *Candle in the Wind* by Elton John ("Goodbye, Norma Jean"). Here, the interval following the unison is slightly different from *Michelle,* a descending major third: as little as needed to convey a very different sense, from now on pervading all the melody and our perception of the song.

Semantic field

When we talk about the semantic field associated to an interval, we are not looking for an exact meaning delivered by that interval, just as if it was a word. We try to assume, rather, that there is a hypothetical general sense, grounding our hypothesis on the examples we know and consider in our analysis. The wider the sample of analysed examples, the more valid our hypothesis will be. Nevetheless, we are not trying to define a fenced and unchangeable field. Instead, the idea is to use this general sense to try and discover how it is shaped, modified, addressed in the way it is used by the different songs and artists we encounter on our journey of analysis.

Coming to the interval of unison, we might summarize a first hypothetical semantic field as: stability, stop, waiting, statement, almost exclamation (further on in this book we will see similarities and differences with the interval of octave in this sense), a stagnation, lack of movement or a barely perceptible movement, sometimes the calm before the storm. Even in the few examples presented here, we can observe the wide variety of possible uses of this semantic field, just by placing more or less wide intervals after the unison, with an ascending or descending movement, with longer or shorter music phrases. And please keep in mind that we have only considered examples in which the melody starts with the unison. We did not analyse the cases (even more countless) where the unison is placed in the middle of a melodic phrase, where it is coloured not only by what follows it, but also by what precedes it. Try to find some examples of this kind, to verify if the semantic fields we are proposing here are still valid and how they are used. Or, try to enlarge the semantic field to embrace new nuances, if you think it is the case. The identification of semantic fields is a very powerful analysis tool, but it is not an exact science. On the contrary, I believe it is even more powerful if you let the personal interpretation in.

As an exercise, try to substitute the second note in *Candle in the Wind* with an ascending fourth, for example: *G#-D#*. You should not alter any other note. What happens to the melody? Now try to substitute the first note, only the first note, in *Michelle*. For example, you can create a descending minor third instead of the unison: *Eb-C*. These simple substituition exercises can tell us much about the musicians' choices and they can teach us much about the intervals we are analysing, besides those chosen for the original melody.

Chapter 3
The seconds

Harmonic minor second

The harmonic minor second measures a distance of just one semitone between two notes. The minor second as a harmonic interval is quite rare. It is easy to imagine that we can find it within a cluster, a set of notes played simultaneously, creating a conglomerate that is usually very dissonant and scarcely harmonious. The cluster can be used as a sudden sense of break or chaos. We can also find a minor second interval inside a chord made of more than three notes, usually in the upper voices. For example, if we build a chord containing the perfect fifth and the minor sixth (e.g. *C-E-G-Ab*), these latter two notes can sometimes be placed close to each other. A sense of dissonance remains anyway, aiming at a resolution in the following chord. This interval can also occur when there's a *suspension*, a technique where you keep a note from the preceding chord while the next chord is forming in the other voices. In our example, we might have a *Ab* that is part of a preceding chord and that is kept while the other voices build the new chord *C major*. Most frequently, this minor sixth resolves descending on the fifth *G*, which is consonant in the new *C major* chord. In gen-

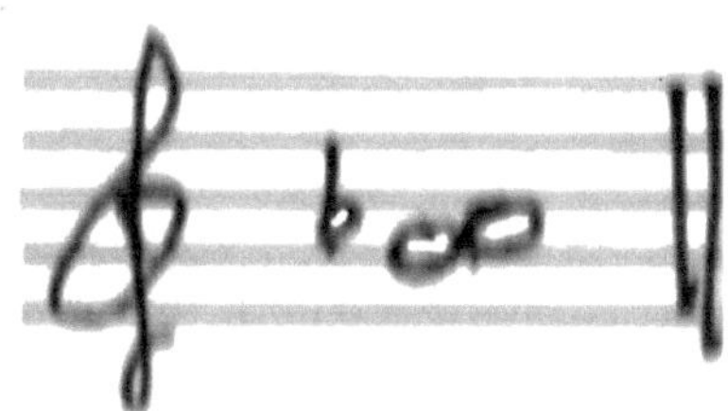

Fig. 14. Harmonic minor second G-Ab.

eral, the most effective resolution of a dissonance is by semitone, by a minor second. In our example, the movement by semitone is a descending one. But in classical harmony the most satisfying resolution by far occurs with an ascending movement by a semitone. This is particularly true when we move from the seventh note of the scale to the octave (or first), stepping up by a semitone. For example, in the classical cadence from the chord on the fifth degree to the chord on the first degree – which in the tonality of *C major* would be the cadence V-I *G major* (*G-B-D*) to *C major* (*C-E-G*) – we find a *B* (third in the *G major* chord) resolving by ascending semitone to *C* (tonic note of the *C major* chord). If we suspend the note *B* in this passage, keeping it while the new *C major* chord is forming, we will have a temporary harmonic minor second between this delayed *B* and the *C* that in the meantime another voice plays to build the new *C major* chord. This *B* will then resolve to another *C* in the voice that delayed with the suspension. This kind of interval sounds much more messy and muddy when it is presented in the lower register. This is why we often find it in the upper voices. Sometimes it is even stretched by an octave, creating a minor ninth interval. Any chord containing the minor ninth, usually together with the minor seventh, is usually a dissonant chord, which creates tension and resolves through a movement by a semitone from the flat ninth.

Melodic minor second

The melodic minor second represents obviously a very small space, the smallest possible. It is also impregnated with a dissonant and tense feeling. All this contributes in making it a sinister and spooky interval. This is particularly evident in the most classical example used to show the minor second features: in the theme from the soundtrack of the movie *The Shark*, written by John Williams in 1975, we notice that the melody obsessively alternate between the two notes of the interval. We never get out of this tunnel that foretells us something sinister is approaching. This insistence contributes to the general sense of claustrophobia, of the threat of something that is about to happen, of growing anxiety. To further enhance these as-

Fig. 15. Theme from the soundtrack of the movie The Shark.

pects, the melody is played on a low register, constantly rising in intensity.

We find a very different situation in the melody of *As Time Goes By* (Herman Hupfeld, 1931), written for a Broadway musical and then used for a movie soundtrack as well, *Casablanca*. This melody starts with an ascending minor second (*G-Ab*), followed by a descent that covers a range of a perfect fourth up to *Eb*, which pivots the melodic movement to end the phrase on *F*, again ascending by a second, but this time a major second. Here, what seems to be the main feature of the general sense is the whole melodic phrase. The phrase is repeated twice, but with important variations: the first time the second note is raised to *Bb* (*G-Bb*, a minor third), together with all the following descending movement, ending with an ascending minor third *F-Ab*. The second repetition starts with a *Bb*, ascends by a fourth to *Eb* and then falls down, ending with an ascending movement from *Bb* to *C*. The first and last interval change, but we clearly hear the same melodic phrase: the same rhythm, the same duration, the same shape. It is not an accident that the descending movement from the second note to the penultimate of the whole phrase remains substantially the same, touching the highest and the lowest notes of the whole melodic phrase, thus defining its overall range. In this reiteration, the most evident feature is the stretching of the first interval: minor second the first time, minor third the second time, perfect fourth the third time. It is a sort of crescendo, built by changing only the first interval of the melodic phrase. The minor second in the first interval appears therefore as a logical choice, since it leaves space

Fig. 16. As Time Goes By, by Herman Hupfeld.

for the crescendo in the following phrases. On the other hand, this interval falls on the first two syllables of the lyrics "You must remember this", somehow highlighting the advice "you must" and stressing the *must* part. In a way, it sounds just as in everyday speech. If we were to say the sentence in our daily life, our intonation might raise a little on the verb 'must' and then come down again. Often melodies and the intervals included in the melodies mimic the way we talk, using the same devices we would use in our everyday life to stress some words or concepts. We will examine this subject in further depth in the next book of this series, *From Intervals to Melody*.

In *A Hard Day's Night* by The Beatles, the melody ("It's been a hard day's night") starts with an ascending minor second interval *B-C*, goes immediately back to the starting note and then remains on a *D* (minor third) repeated three times (unison). The second melodic phrase that closes the melodic arch starts instead from *D*, goes up to *E* (ascending major second) and then moves in a wider and more varied fashion compared to the incipit ("And I've been working like a dog"). Here, we might assume that the note *C* in the minor second movement *B-C-B* is a pivot, almost just a passing note. Yet, if we compare it to the static three unison notes at the end of the first melodic phrase, this interval appears animated and connotative. In this case, this very little movement, just one semitone, stresses the sensation that the events the lyrics are talking about have just happened, that the time lapse since the narrated events is really tiny, though it is worded in the past ("It's been a"). Just as the long notes on the following unisons give us the sensation of the boredom of long hours of work ("hard day's night"). Comparing it to the variation of ascending major second in the second melodic phrase, we might interpret our interval as a sort of preparation, a hesitant movement that prepares the more confident motion of the concluding phrase.

Stevie Wonder's *Isn't She Lovely?* as well presents a melody that starts with a minor second interval coming immediately back to the

Fig. 17. The Beatles, A Hard Day's Night.

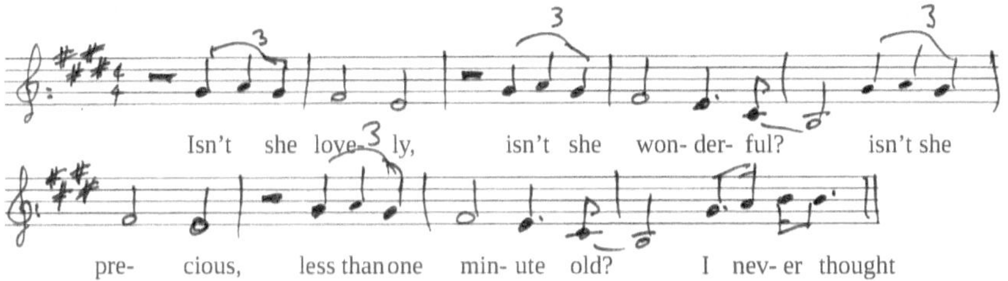

Fig. 18. Stevie Wonder, Isn't She Lovely?

first note (*G#-A-G#*). The phrase then ends with long and descending notes. Here again we find a sort of pivot on the note *A*, enlarging the range of the whole melodic phrase to a descending perfect fourth (*A-E*) the first time, and to an octave (*A-A*) the second time. There is a sort of mimic of speech in this case as well, since the minor second interval falls on the interrogative part of the sentence ("Isn't she"), just as we might do in our everyday life if we wanted to stress the rethorical sense of the question. The melodic phrase is reiterated here as well: the first time spanning a perfect fourth, the second time spanning an octave with a longer phrase, the third time again spanning a perfect fourth, the fourth time again spanning an octave. So, when the fifth melodic phrase comes, the small variation in its attack is enough to tell us that something changed, that the reasoning is coming to its conclusion: here, the ascending minor second interval is followed by another ascending major second interval. What before was a soft ascent followed by a descent, here is presented as a real ascent in small steps ("I never thought").

Another example I'd like to give is the melody at the beginning of *White Christmas* (Irving Berlin, 1954). Here the minor second interval appears immediately, on the second note, falling on the word "dreaming" ("I'm dreaming of a white Christmas"). Again, the

Fig. 19. White Christmas, *by Irving Berlin.*

melody then comes immediately back to the starting note (*E-F-E*), but the melody moves slower, almost as if it was slowed down, as in a dream. The beginning of the whole melody moves by minor second intervals: from *E* to *F*, from *F* to *E*, from *E* to *D#* and then again upwards from *D#* to *E* and from *E* to *F*. The overall range of the melodic phrase is rather small, just a major second (*F* is the higher note, *D#* the lowest). And in the conclusion of the melodic phrase, again we find just two notes, *F#* and *G*, separated by an ascending minor second. Only in the second phrase does the melody lift off, opening up to a scale-like movement involving major second intervals (wider than before) and a range of a perfect fifth, touching a high note on *D* and a low note on *G*. So, the first melodic phrase is built around the smallest possible interval and a very small range. This amplifies the effect of opening in the next phrase, that involves wider intervals and a wider range. At the same time, it seems that we can assume a general sense of dream, of unreal, associated with the minor second interval, especially when it is repeated both ascending and descending. Probably, this aspect is partly connected with its tense nature, almost something imperfect as compared to the major second interval, which in general sounds less dissonant.

Up to now we only presented examples with melodies starting with an ascending minor second. So I think it is fair to quote a couple of melodies that start with a descending minor second. The first one is Beethoven's *Für Elise* (1810). Here again the minor second interval is repeated before the melody opens up with wider intervals, that appear stronger and more meaningful in contrast with the previous minor second interval. The general sense seems to be again associated to the idea of dreaming, but here we find a stronger tendency towards melancholy, due to the downward direction of the interval, instead of the ascending movement of the previous examples.

Selene by Gong starts with a descending melody by a minor second *E-D#*. This second note is held longer, before proceeding its de-

Fig. 20. Beethoven, Für Elise.

Fig. 21. Gong, Selene.

scent down to the lower perfect fourth *B*. At the end of the melodic phrase, we find instead an ascending scale starting from *G#*, that expands the range of the melody to an overall minor sixth. This general range of minor sixth is clearly the most connotative interval of this invocation of the 'spirit of the moon'. The first descending movement by a semitone, though, is also relevant, since it sets the tone of sweetness and a downward direction that starts with an intimate movement: as if to say that the smallest distance of a semitone is the one that better covers the immense distance that separates us from the moon! Should we change that second note with a *D*, a descending major second, the mood of the melody would completely change.

Semantic field

The minor second interval covers a very small distance, therefore it basically conveys a sense of very small movement, a very small time lapse or space, intimacy. It also mimics the inflections of a speech when we try to stress something. In addition, its dissonant, tense character might be emphatised to convey a sense of imminent danger, instability, unbalance, or the idea of dream, of something that is just beyond our reach, just a semitone away... Wether it is placed within a harmonic or melodic movement, its dissonant tendency is to resolve to the nearest semitone, preferably ascending but sometimes even descending. From a melodic point of view, the minor second is a strong feature of the phrygian mode scale: the scale S-T-T-T-S-T-T built starting from *E* in the key of *C major* (*E-F-G-A-B-C-D-E*). The passage from the first to the second note is a semitone, an ascending minor second interval. In the ancient times, the phrygian mode scale was considered to be very lascivious. It was thought to be so powerful that it could corrupt even the most hardened soldier's spirit. Of course, the phrygian scale of those times was not the same as the one we call phrygian mode today. But I think we can assume among the minor second's semantic fields a certain undertone of sensuality as well.

As an exercise, try to substitute the second note, and only that note, in the melodies of *A Hard Day's Night* and of *Isn't She Lovely?* Better if you use notes that are very far away from the first note, maybe even with a descending interval. Once you have tried this, it should be clear to you that this interval is not a simple accident in those melodies. It is rather a specific need of the melodic line in both songs.

What about changing the second note in Beethoven's *Für Elise*? Let's say we put a descending perfect fourth instead of the minor second. Finally, let's take the melody of *White Christmas* as well and let's try the same experiment. Here, the whole first part moves by minor seconds, but changing the first interval should be enough to have an idea of the effect. Maybe we could substitute it with a wider interval, for example a perfect fifth (*E-B-E-D#-E*).

Harmonic major second

The major second interval covers a distance of one tone, that is two semitones. It shares many features with the minor second for obvious reasons: small distance, small movement, harmonic gravitation towards the tonic note of the melody. From a harmonic point of view, this is still a dissonant interval, though there is less tension here compared to the minor second, with a slightly 'harsher' tone in the resolution movement. Its resolving tendency leads more by semitone towards the minor third than by tone towards the tonic, though there are many examples of this latter kind. Also, in this case we find this

Fig. 22. Harmonic major interval G-A.

interval more easily in the middle or higher voices: a chord containing a major second interval from its tonic will be usually considered a ninth chord, with the characteristic jump to the higher octave (in the second interval *C-D*, *D* is raised by an octave, changing the interval into a ninth). The ninth chord results from the principle of tertiary harmony of stacking thirds: *C-E* (major third), *E-G* (minor third), *G-B* (major third) and *B-D* (minor third). We can find a peculiar harmonic use of the major second in the so called *backdoor resolution*, mainly in blues progressions. Essentially, it is a final cadence in a harmonic phrase, where we get back to the tonic chord, the first degree of the key, the most resolutive and conclusive chord, arriving from the chord built on the minor seventh degree. For example, in the key of *C major*, the backdoor resolution would occur if we create a chord sequence that ends with the movement from *Bb major* to *C major*. This movement VII-VIII creates a major second interval between these two chords and their tonic notes, resolving the tension by tone rather than by semitone.

While the minor second interval keeps a certain amount of dissonance in the tension by semitone that it creates in relation to the tonic note, even when it is in a ninth chord, the dissonant feature of the major second is much softer. The ninth chord, though it is considered to be dissonant, often a dominant chord that must resolve on a more conclusive and relaxed chord, is anyway the result of stacking alternating thirds (major and minor) over each other. This gives it a reassuring sound, which our ear has learnt to accept. In the same way, its role in a resolving movement like the blues backdoor resolution makes our ear perceive it as a not-so-strong dissonance, provided that it resolves quickly, with a movement by tone that is less tense than the movement by semitone.

Melodic major second

The small distance and the small movement are still the main features of the major second interval in the context of a melody. Specifically, one of its strongest semantic features involves the movement of the scale, a direction in small steps. This makes it very similar to the minor second interval. Here, though, we can have two major second intervals one after the other without breaking the pattern of the scale, without falling into a cromatic movement by semitones. For example, this melodic movement by tones was characteristic of the vocal church music in the Medieval times, like in the so called Gregorian chant. In the 20th century it gained new relevance in the melodic movements of the experimental music, from serialism to Messiaen's modes of limited transposition, a technique recently also used by bands like Cardiacs. Yet the major second interval provides us with an unexpected abundance of senses and creative possibilities.

In *Autumn Leaves* (Joseph Kosma, 1945), all the melodic phrases are built as a sequence of ascending major second intervals, followed by a jump by an ascending perfect fourth (the first phrase starts from *E*, goes up to *F#*, then to *G* and from there it jumps to *C*). The sequence of the first three notes conveys the idea of a movement by scale, a step by step rise, preparing and highlighting the conclusive jump by perfect fourth. The overall range of the melodic phrase covers a minor sixth (*E-C*). The ascending major second interval, in this case, is strongly affected by the direction of the scale and by the overall range of a minor sixth of the melodic phrase.

In *Silent Night* (Frank Xaver Gruber, 1818), the melody starts with long notes on *G*, interrupted by an upward movement to *A*. The phrase then ends with a descending jump by a minor third to *E*. The slow movement contributes to the sense of silence, immobility, of the particular calm you feel after it has snowed. Breaking this atmosphere with a larger interval (let's say beyond the third) or with a dissonant interval (even the minor second) would be detrimental. So here comes our major second, that also plays another role: extending the range of the whole melody to a perfect fourth (*A* is the higher note, *E* the lower

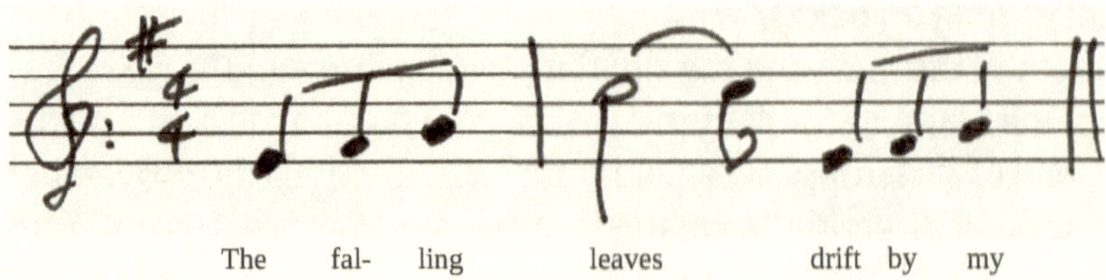

Fig. 23. Autumn Leaves, *by Joseph Kosma.*

Fig. 24. Silent Night, *by Frank Xaver Gruber.*

note). Actually, try to take the second note awway from the melody, keeping only the notes *G-G-E*. Now the overall range is a minor third and the effect is completely different! Try now to substitute the note *A* with a *F* or a *Ab*. In both cases, the result is totally different, even if we change just one apparently irrelevant note!

One of the examples most frequently used to explain the major second interval, in this case descending, is *Yesterday* by The Beatles. The melody here starts with a descending major second interval (*G-F-F*), followed by a break, a pause. A short melodic phrase built only using our major second interval, and isolated from the rest of the melody. This isolation highlights and amplifies the effect of that interval. We might associate this descending major second to a gesture of bending our head to the side, as if to say 'too bad!' or 'what a memory!'. A sad memory, where this sadness is mainly created by the descending direction of the interval. Musicologist David Bennett, in one of his Youtube videos (*Does Everyone Play Yesterday Wrong?*, https://www.youtube.com/watch?v=pOtcLmOeScM), analyzed Paul McCartney's vocal performance on this passage, highlighting the almost microtonal descent of the voice, that leans on the final *F* starting

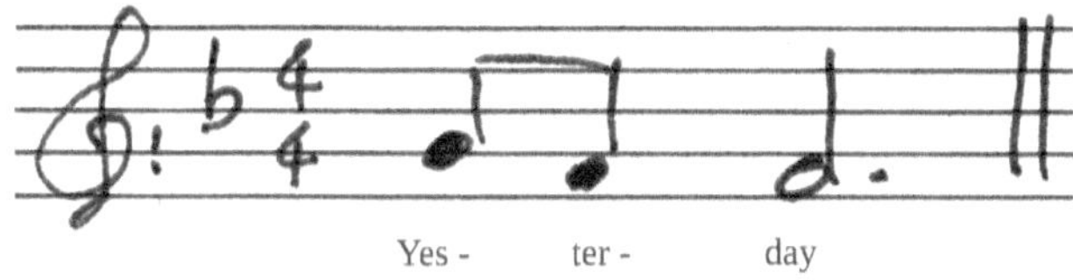

Fig. 25. The Beatles, Yesterday.

Fig. 26. David Bowie, Space Oddity.

from a note that is definetely below the *G* and slightly above the *F*. We talk about microtonal intervals when the distance between the notes is less than the measuring unit of a semitone. We will be talking again about them in chapter 10. The use of the descending major second interval associated to sad memory is a recurring theme and we will look at it in more depth in the next book *From Intervals to Melody*.

A slighlty different instance is presented in David Bowie's *Space Oddity*. Here, we find the descending major second, the 'sad memory' interval, over a lyrics that seems to say something completely different: "Ground control to Major Tom". It is a radio communication between the launching base and the astronaut in the rocket that is about to lift off. Therefore, we might assume an atmosphere full of fervent expectation, hope, the beginning of an adventure towards the unknown. Instead, Bowie decides to insert this humble, almost resigned interval, making us prefigure from the very first notes of the melody the tragic ending of the story.

In AC/DC's *It's a Long Way to the Top (If You Wanna Rock'n'Roll)*, the whole melody on the verses is built around the

Fig. 27. AC/DC, It's a Long Way To The Top (If You Wanna Rock'n'roll).

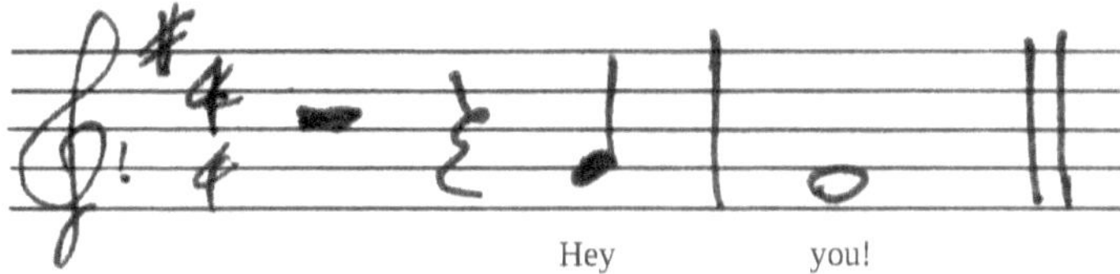

Fig. 28. Pink Floyd, Hey You.

major second interval *Ab-Bb*. The words are a list of the many strug-
gles and pains of a rock band before they reach the fame: "Riding
down the highway / Going to a show / Stop in all the byways / playing rock and roll" in the first verse, while in the second verse "Hotel,
motel / make you wanna cry / Lady do the hard sell / Know the reason why". These two alternating notes, in a small range, give us the
idea of repetition and of being trapped in a pain chain. The same
repetition, but with a wider interval, might convey the sensation of
wider spaces and better chances to get out of it. Then the verse ends
with more quick and rhythmic phrases, before getting to the refrain
that contains the title of the song.

Hey You by Pink Floyd starts with a descending major second interval *G-A*, exactly on the exhortation "Hey you!". A call, of course,
but to someone close. It is not a shout to someone far away, where a
wider interval would be more fitting. On the contrary, this is a small
vocal gesture, as if to talk to someone in the same room.

In *My Funny Valentine*, written by Richard Rodgers and Lorenz
Hart in 1937 for the musical *Babes in Arms*, the melody always
moves by major seconds: *C-D-E-D-E-D* ("My funny Valentine").
This melodic movement is intimate, small, tender but not so sad: the

Fig. 29. My Funny Valentine, *by Rodgers e Hart.*

melody direction tends upwards. The small range of the intervals is also a sort of preparation for the jump to the ascending perfect fifth *C-G* in the third repetition of the melodic phrase, on the word "smile" ("you make me smile").

Semantic field

The second interval is a small interval, suggesting a small movement, a tight space, intimacy, introspection. Or indicating a step in a certain direction, a step up, or down. While a minor second conveys a stronger tension downward, the major second communicates a more assertive, less uncertain sense, pointing more upwards.

From a harmonic point of view, it is a dissonant interval anyway, that creates a certain tension towards a resolving point. This resolving point, though, is usually different in a minor interval and a major interval. And the major interval can actually resolve moving through a whole tone, instead of a semitone. This creates a less strong effect in the dynamic tension-resolution. At the same time, though, it can be used to communicate a stronger stability in the harmonic and melodic movements.

As a melodic interval, we can say that it is strongly affected by the direction it takes. We saw that a descending second interval, both minor and major, conveys a sense of sadness, introspection, often connected with the theme of memory. The minor interval appears to be more uncertain, a deviation from the main road, or the hesitant start of a direction. The major interval, on the other hand, is sadder, almost accepting the inevitable. But if the same interval takes an ascending direction, the picture significantly changes. The effect is more similar to a list, a more confident step in a direction, presenting for sure a bigger openness compared to the minor interval.

Here as well, as an exercise, try to substitute one note of the interval in the suggested examples. For instance, the major second in *Yesterday* could be changed into a perfect fifth, still descending: *G-C-C*. Or we might try to simply change the interval direction, to verify how the effect changes: *G-A-A*.

We could do the same with *Space Oddity*: what happens if we change the major seconpd interval into a third, or a fifth for example?

And what if we change direction, turning it into an ascending major second?

How much would the sense of the melody change in *Hey You* if the second note was a *C*, for example, instead of a *F*, with a much wider range?

<h1>Chapter 4</h1>
<h1>The thirds</h1>

Harmonic minor third

The minor third interval covers a distance of one tone and a half, that is three semitones. From a harmonic point of view, nowadays it is considered to be a consonant interval, since it is the basis in the building of the minor chord triad (for instance *C-Eb-G*). The tone of this chord is usally considered to be sad, as compared to the major chord, which instead is built starting from a major third interval. To understand its sad and humble effect, it might be useful to keep in mind the semantic field of its inversion, the major sixth (see chapter 7 in this book). In the end, the use of inversions in harmonic movements is a common practice, which is often needed to ensure that all the voices are moving correctly. In tertiary harmony, where we stack thirds to build up chords, by stacking two minor thirds over each other (instead of alternating minor and major thirds) we get the diminished triad (*C-Eb-Gb*), a dissonant chord with a very strong tension. If we want to add another third, we are faced with two important choices. If we add a major third we get the so called semi-diminished chord, often notated as 5b/7 (*C-Eb-Gb-Bb*). If instead we add another minor third, we get the seventh diminished chord (*C-Eb-Gb-Bbb*, or if you prefer *C-Eb-Gb-A*). In this chord, all the notes are a minor

Fig. 30. The harmonic minor third interval G-Bb.

third apart from each other, therefore it is impossible to say which one is the real tonic of the chord. This peculiar chord resolves the tension by shifting any of its chord tones by a semitone, usually with an ascending movement. This feature made it a very important chord in the history of harmony, especially for the decisive role it played in the fall of harmony. The use of this chord in Wagner's *Siegfried* is often suggested as the definitive moment of crisis of classical harmony. We should say that in that particular case there were also other elements at play, like the peculiar distribution of the notes in the different voices, one of the first examples of quartal harmony. Moreover, Wagner himself already often used this diminished chord as a sort of springboard to modulate to different and sometimes unexpected tonalities.

The minor third interval can also be found in the seventh chord (a major chord with a minor seventh: *C-E-G-Bb*). This time it is located between the last two notes (*G-Bb*). In this major chord, often also called dominant chord, the minor seventh *Bb* is considered dissonant, with a strong harmonic tension to resolve up a semitone.

Melodic minor third

The minor third interval still presents quite a small range, associated with intimacy, small spaces and lullabies, when it is not used to build arpeggios on the chord tones in the melodic movements.

In *A Day in the Life* by The Beatles, the melody starts with an ascending minor third (on the first two syllables of the verse "I read the news today oh boy"). Then it goes back to the starting note, expanding the range of the melodic phrase at the end (*B-D-B-E-B-D-E-B*). The tone of the melody resembles almost a singsong, as if to stress the daily routine of reading the news every morning.

Fig. 31. *The Beatles*, A Day in the Life.

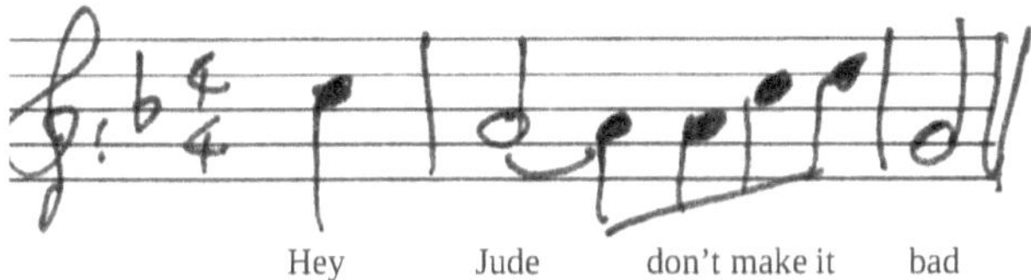

Fig. 32. The Beatles, Hey Jude.

In *Hey Jude,* again by The Beatles, we instead immediately find a descending minor third *C-A* ("Hey Jude"). Here, this interval softens the call in a sort of intimacy, a persuading tone, completely different from Pink Floyd's exclamatory "Hey you".

In the chorus of King Crimson's *I Talk to the Wind,* the melody starts with a jump by an ascending minor third *G#-B* ("I talk"). Here we can see that the minor third is the minum size needed to create a jump, rather than a step. The smallest jump, we might say. An intimate jump, that somehow corresponds to the idea of talking to the wind, an open dialogue with the external world, and yet an inner and intimate dialogue.

Fig. 33. King Crimson, I Talk to the Wind.

Black Sabbath's *Iron Man*'s melody follows the guitar and bass riff step by step at the beginning. It starts with our ascending minor third interval and then proceeds ascending to the perfect fourth: *B-*

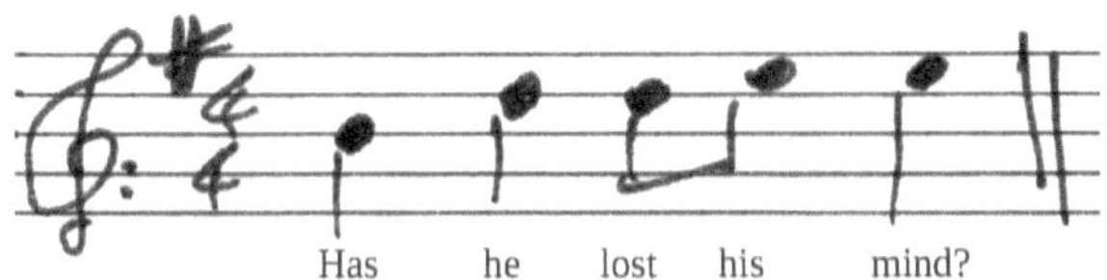

Fig. 34. Black Sabbath, Iron Man.

Fig. 35. Black Sabbath, Black Sabbath.

D-D-E-E ("Has he lost his mind?"). The minor tone of this interval conveys a certain sense of evil, the idea that there is something not quite right and that it might be dangerous as well. The ascending direction of the melody contributes in conveying this general sense: if we tried to change the direction downwards, we'd probably get a sadder and more tender sense. At the same time, the minor third interval, the overall range of the whole melodic phrase and the ascending direction, all follow the questioning tone of the lyrics.

In a similar way, the melody in *Black Sabbath*, again by Black Sabbath, begins with a phrase with a range of a minor third on the question "What is this". To be precise, here we have a step by step movement, passing through a major second and then a minor second: *G-A-Bb*. This example allows us to underline the importance of considering not only the intervals in isolation, but also the range covered by the whole melodic phrase in the analysis of melodies. In the end, this ascending major second plays the role of a step, a small step indicating a direction and taking us gradually to the minor third. Again, the minor tone of this third conveys a sense of distress, of something sinister hidden behind the question "What is this that stands before me?".

Lullaby by The Cure presents a minor third interval *G#-B*, as the basis on which the whole melody develops on the first two phrases.

Fig. 36. The Cure, Lullaby.

This is an example of singsong, typical of many lullabies and nursery rhymes, where we often find the third interval. Here, the choice of a minor third, instead of a major third, supports the gloomy sense of a sort of nightmare in which the protagonist of the lyrics is a prey in a spider's web. But, as the title says, it is anyway a lullaby, in a metaphorical sense as well.

Semantic field

While second intervals, both major and minor, are more or less small steps, the minor third interval is the first interval that we can call a jump, a small jump, the smallest possible jump. In this sense, it still maintains a quite small, intimate, introspective, maybe held back feel. It is actually a consonant interval, but in its minor version it is possible to accentuate its sad and gloomy aspects to convey melancholy, or instead expectations of evil and danger. Third intervals are often used for their singsong character, as in a nursery rhyme, a lullaby, or as in a list. The choice of the minor version colours this intention with a sad, gloomy, sinister atmosphere. The same minor third interval, though, especially when it is descending, conveys a sense of intimacy, closeness, maybe even tenderness, compared to the major version.

As an exercise, try to substitute the minor third interval in the examples provided with a major third interval, and compare the result with the original melody.

In *A Day in the Life*, try to change it with a wider jump, maybe a perfect fifth *B-F#*. Listen how a simple shifting of a single note can change the overall tone of the whole melody.

In *Hey Jude*, try to substitute the minor third with an octave, or a unison: how does the perception of space change? Who are we talking to now? Are we talking to someone next to us, with a persuading tone, or to a far away person, calling for his attention, maybe to prevent an imminent danger?

Harmonic major third

From a harmonic point of view, the same considerations made for the minor third are still valid: it is a consonant interval, the basis for the building of the major chord. The general character of the major third and of the chord it generates is more cheerful, open, joyful, compared to the minor third.

Still keeping in mind the differences in the characters of the minor and major versions, the third interval is often used in vocal or instrumental harmonizations, over the main vocal or a riff. In general, the result is a consonant expansion of the melodic range. This device is often used when we need to give a more open and full character to a certain musical section, like a chorus. When we harmonize with a major third, the cheerful and affermative tone of the interval will affect the main melody as well.

The third can also be the interval between chords in a chord sequence. This has had a peculiar relevance in the history of music since the second half of the 19th century. Music theory in that period produced the idea of a harmonic analysis based on the functions of each chord within a context. Riemann, specifically, identified three main functions and four secondary functions within the context of a given key. The basic assumption was that if two triads share two common notes out of three, their function can not be perceived too different within the same context, or tonality. All the chords sharing two notes out of three are separated by a third. For instance, if we take the *C major* chord (*C-E-G*) and the *E minor* chord (*E-G-B*), we can see that the notes are almost the same, these chords are made of the same matter. So, composers like Franz Schubert and Robert Schumann started to experiment, using mainly chord sequences by thirds. Or maybe they started experimenting and Riemann just aknowledged them: in the end, theory comes after practice and tries to explain it, not the other way round. In most recent times, follow-

Fig. 37. The harmonic major third interval G-B.

ing slighlty different paths and reasonings, these chord sequences by thirds, especially major thirds, became a standard in most of the psychedelic music. For instance, Pink Floyd used them a lot: most of the verse in *High Hopes* is built on two chords, *C minor* and *Ab major*, separated by an ascending major third. *Welcome to the Machine* is entirely built on alternating *C major* and *E minor*, again separated by a major third. And we can find movements by thirds in many other songs within the harmonic sequence. Many Porcupine Tree songs present relevant harmonic movements by thirds as well. In *Trains* the chord sequence goes as follows: *D major - C major - E minor* (ascending major third) - *A major - A minor - C major* (ascending major third) - *F major - D major* (descending minor third). *Shesmovedon* starts with a movement from *E minor* to *G major* (ascending minor third). In *Russia on Ice* we find the sequence *E minor - C major* (descending major third) - *D major - Bb major* (descending major third) - *Eb major*. In *Moon Touches Your Shoulder* the harmonic sequence ends with the movements from *D major* to *F# minor* (ascending major third) and then to *A minor* (ascending minor third). *Brainstorm* by Hawkwind starts with a movement from *A major* to *C major* (ascending minor third). At the beginning of *Zero the Hero and the Witch's Spell* by Gong, we find the movement *B major - D# minor* (ascending major third), while at the end of the harmonic sequence we find the movement from *G# minor* to *B major* (ascending minor third). *Opium for the People* by Planet Gong goes from *G# minor* to *B major* (ascending minor third), then from *C# major* to *E major* (ascending minor third), then to *G# major* (ascending major third), then again from *F# major* to *A major* (ascending minor third), from *G major* to *E minor* (descending minor third), to *C# minor* (descending minor third) and again from *F major* to *D# major* (descending minor third). You can find a lot of other examples in bands like Here and Now, where many harmonic sequences are built on the chord tones of a starting chord, therefore almost always a third apart from each other.

Melodic major third

The major third interval covers a distance of two tones, or four semitones. The major third as well can be repeated several times to

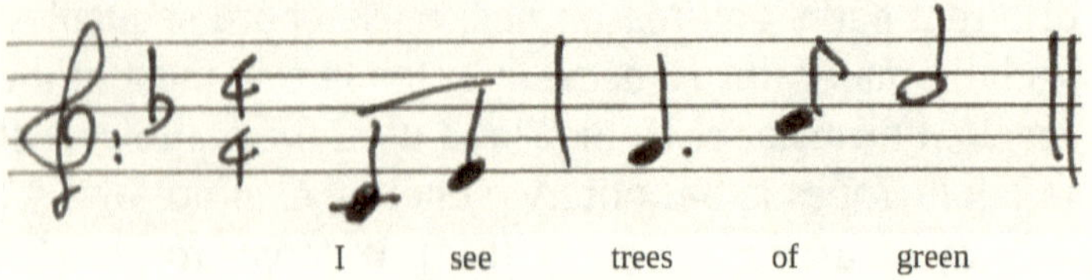

Fig. 38. What a Wonderful World, *by George Douglas.*

create the effect of a singsong: lullabies, nursery rhymes, lists. Compared to the minor third, it is wider, more open, joyful, cheerful.

The melody in *What a Wonderful World* (George Douglas, 1967), a song made famous by Louis Armstrong's interpretation, starts with an ascending phrase *C-E-F-A-C* ("I see trees of green"). We can spot our major third interval between the first two notes *C* and *E* and between *F* and *A*. The direction, always ascending, of the melodic phrase conveys the joy for what we are seing, but it is already the first major third interval that gives us the idea of a wonderful world.

In *Morning Has Broken* by Cat Stevens, we find a sequence of thirds (*C-E-G*) in the first phrase, ending then with a movement from *C* to *D*. Here we can consider the first jump by a major third as the beginning of an arpeggio, where the chord tones of *C major* are played one at a time. In fact, the following notes are *G* and again *C* one octave higher. The melody lands up to *D* in the higher octave, defining a very large range, a ninth. We get the image of an opening, the rising of the sun, the immensity of nature, from this short melodic phrase. And the major third at the beginning of the phrase is relevant in conveying this sense: it wouldn't be the same if it was a minor third or a smaller interval.

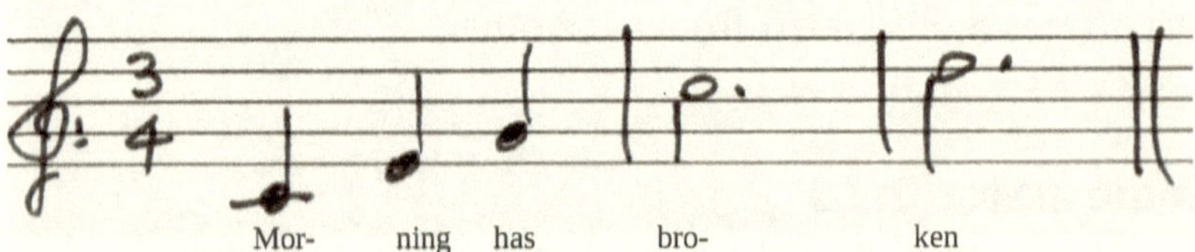

Fig. 39. Cat Stevens, Morning Has Broken.

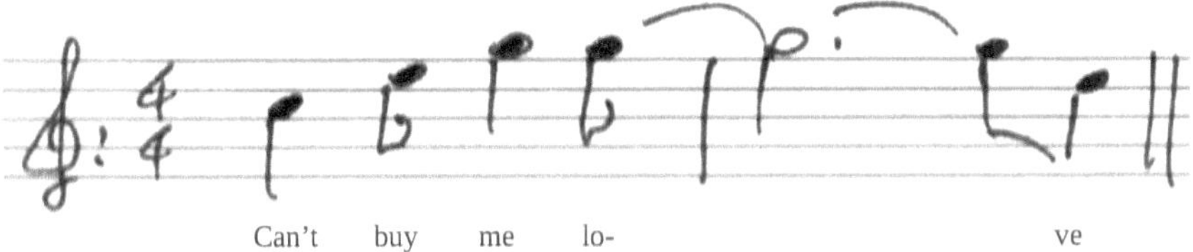

Fig. 40. The Beatles, Can't Buy Me Love.

Can't Buy Me Love by The Beatles starts with the melody of the refrain ("Can't buy me love"), again with a *C major* arpeggio: *C-E-G-G-E*. The major third at the start of the movement is again a chord tone, a harmonious, cheerful, open passage. In this case I would say affirmative and lighthearted. It is a passage needed to arrive to the fifth of the chord, *G*, that defines the overall range of the melody, which then ends descending again by a minor third on *E*.

In *Obladi Oblada*, again by The Beatles, we find the major third interval in the chorus. Again, it is an arpeggio on the chord tones of a *Bb minor* chord (*Bb-D-F*). Here again I think the main effect is the sense of a lighthearted line.

Another example of an ascending third used in a melody shaped as an arpeggio is *When the Saints Go Marching In*, a traditional spiritual gospel from New Orleans, again made famous by Louis Armstrong's interpretation.

On the other hand, *Summertime*, written by George Gershwin in 1935 for the opera *Porgy and Bess*, immediately presents a major third at the beginning of the melody, but this time is a descending third. It is nothing more than a quick gesture, since the melody immediately goes back to the starting note. It is enough, though, to con-

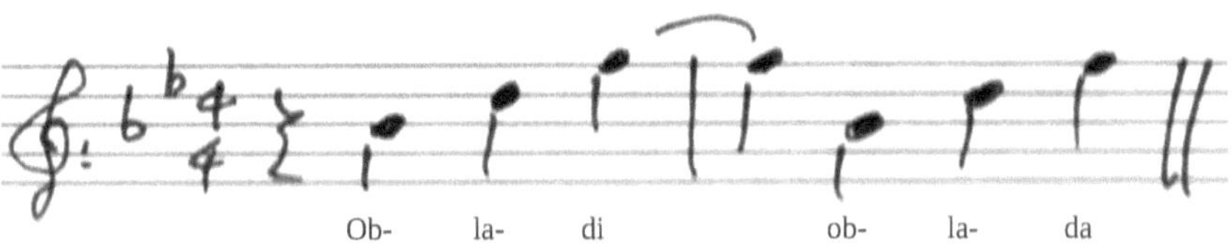

Fig. 41. The Beatles, Obladi Oblada.

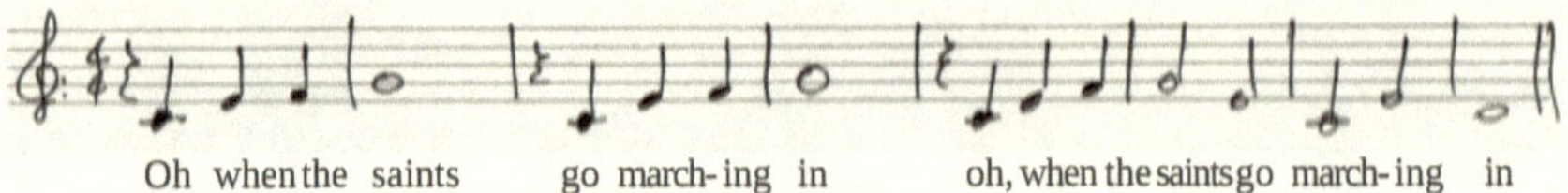

Fig. 42. When the Saints Go Marching In.

vey a sense of tenderness, of a pleasant memory, of the touch of a warm breeze. This strong difference with the sense we found up to now for the major third is due to the descending direction of the interval. Please note that in the famous version recorded by Janis Joplin this interval has been changed to an ascending major second. Janis Joplin herself, though, in her live performances, went often back to the original interval. This is maybe one of the rarest cases of substitution of an interval at the beginning of a melody that is successful and functional. Nonetheless, the sense of the melodic passage gets deeply altered together with the interval.

Semantic field

Once again, we are faced with an interval that depicts a small jump, a jump though that is already wide enough to give impetus to joy, to the brightness and the magnificence of the universe. The major third as well can be used to create singsong melodies, with all the possible senses and meanings that we can associate to them. But the major third, especially when it is ascending, suits perfectly melodic movements by arpeggio on a given chord. This chord will necessarily be major, therefore happy, cheerful. In this kind of melodic move-

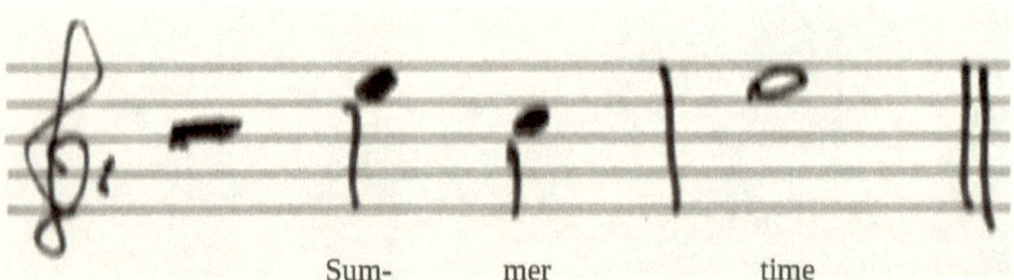

Fig. 43. Summertime, by George Gershwin.

ments, the phrase usually follows a curve, descending again before the end; or, when it goes on ascending, it often generates extremely wide melodic ranges. These two possibilities will have a strong impact on the semantic field delivered by the major third interval. Another aspect that has an evident impact on the sense conveyed by this interval is its direction. An ascending melodic movement will highlight its open, cheerful, joyful character. In a descending melodic movement, instead, the sweeter and softer character will emerge.

If we try to substitute the second note in *What a Wonderful World* with a *G* (ascending perfect fifth), we can hear all the difference that a single different note can make in a melody. The same applies obviously for all the other examples in this chapter.

The case of Janis Joplin's version of *Summertime* proves though that it is not impossible to find a substitute interval which, while conveying a different sense, will fit the mood of the melody and the interpretation we want to give of the song.

Chapter 5
The fourth

T he perfect fourth interval covers a distance of two tones and a half, that is five semitones. All the perfect intervals can be altered downward to get a diminished interval, or upward to get an augmented, or extended, interval. The diminished fourth interval (two tones, or four semitones) is an enharmonic equivalent of the major third. The augmented fourth interval (three tones, or six semitones) is an enharmonic equivalent of the diminished fifth. In this illustration of the various intervals, I chose to use the most commonly used definition to name the enharmonic equivalents: in the case of a separation by two tones, the interval will be called major third instead of diminished fourth; in the case of a separation by three tones, the interval will be called diminished fifth instead of augmented fourth. Some speficic cases, though, can make the reason clear why we have these enharmonic equivalents and show some characteristic connotations of the diminished and augmented fourth intervals.

Since the beginning of the 20th century, a scale made of eight notes, instead of the usual seven, entered in the Western compositional practice and then in musical theory: the octatonic scale. It is a scale based on a matrix diminished seventh chord (1-3b-5b-7b, for

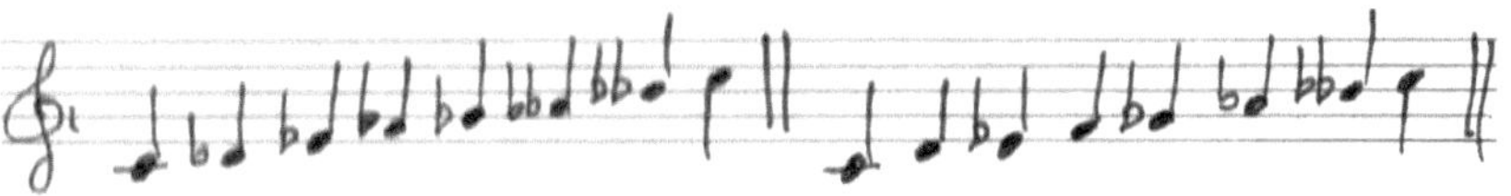

Fig. 44. The two possible octatonic scales: S-T-S-T-S-T-S or T-S-T-S-T-S-T.

example *C-Eb-Gb-Bbb* or *A*). In the sequence of the notes, semitones and tones alternate, starting from the first or from the latter, in the only variation possible. In the octatonic scale starting with the semitone interval, or minor second, we find the following sequence of intervals in relation to the starting note: minor second (*C-Db*), minor third (*C-Eb*), diminished fourth (*C-Fb*) and so on. So, here is our diminished fourth interval, appearing here because we already used the third interval, necessarily as a minor third.

The scale we can build starting from the fourth note of a major scale is called lydian mode: using the notes from the *C major* scale, it would be the scale built starting from *F*. Here, the fourth note of the scale is three tones away from the tonic note of the scale, therefore we will call it augmented fourth. The interval comes after the (major) third and is followed by the perfect fifth interval. So it could not take any other name than fourth, in this case augmented fourth. In addition, the presence of a perfect fifth here suggests that we can not use the name of diminished fifth for this interval, because it would be confusing.

Harmonic perfect fourth

The perfect fourth interval is usually considered as a consonant interval, yet with some problematic aspects. In ancient times, it was a reference interval, and that's why we call it 'perfect' still today. Its inversion is a perfect fifth, that is a consonant interval as well. But since the thirds became consonant intervals, they started overshadowing the idea that there could not be any tension inside the perfect fourth interval. When two notes appear at a reciprocal dis-

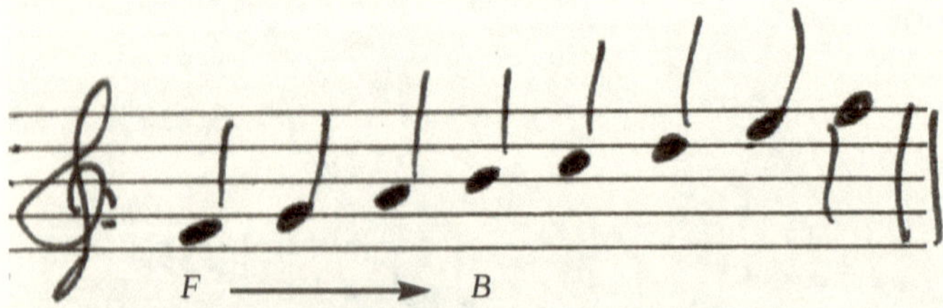

Fig. 45.The lydian scale starting from F includes the interval F-B, which in this case is called augmented fourth.

Fig. 46. The perfect fourth interval G-C.

tance of a perfect fourth, in two different voices, we feel a consonant harmony, partly because the perfect fourth is associated to its inversion, the fifth, one of the most consonant intervals of all. But as soon as we put the same interval in the movement of the voices, it will result rather harsh, provided it is not the resolving point of a tension. And it can appear even harsher if the voices keep moving maintaining the distance of a perfect fourth between them (parallel fourths). To tell the truth, these harmonizing techniques are still in use in several folk traditions. In rock and pop muisic we can find parallel fourths harmonizations over a riff, but only rarely in the vocal harmonizations.

As a harmonic movement of chords, the passage from the I degree to the IV is worth mentioning. Within a key, these are two formally identical major chords. Since the fourth interval is an inversion of the fifth, we won't be able to identify the real relationship between these two chords, until the arrival of a third chord, or of a revealing note in the movements of the parts. For example, in an obstinately repeated passage between the *C major* chord and the *F major* chord, our ear can not decide whether it is a movement from the I to the IV degree in the key of *C major*, or if it is a movement from the V to the I degree in the key of *F major*. This ambivalent harmonic relation has often been exploited, especially in songwriters' compositions, keeping that tension until a dominant chord (*G major* in the key of *C major*), or a subdominant chord (*Bb* in the key of *F major*) appears. A more elegant solution is including the fourth note of the scale on the chord that has the function of subdominant on the IV degree (*B* in the *F major* chord, if this is the IV degree), or the (minor) seventh note of the scale built on the V degree (*Bb* in the *C major* chord, if this is the V degree). It can even be a passing note, a quick hint: our ear will be anyway able to seize the clue and decode the relationship. In many Beatles' songs we find similar solutions, with the revealing notes hidden in the bass line.

From a harmonic point of view, we mentioned that the fourth is an inversion of the fifth. The perfect fourth interval will therefore be present in any inverted chord: if we take a *C major* chord (*C-E-G*) and we build its first inversion (*E-G-C*), we find a perfect fourth between *G* and *C*. In the same way, if we build the second inversion, taking *E* as well to the higher octave (*G-C-E*), the perfect fourth interval stays the same between *G* and *C*.

There are then more hard cases, where it is difficult to claim that the interval is consonant. One of these cases is the so called suspended chord, usually notated as sus4. It is a triad in which the third is substituted by a perfect fourth: in the *C major* chord, *E* would be substituted by *F*. This substitution can be treated as a delaying note, having a major (or less frequently minor) chord on the same tonic following the sus4, resolving the tension to a third. Or it can be used as an independent chord, even at the end of a cadence, to give a sense of suspension and opening to the harmonic conclusion. This very same chord, in addition, can be the basis of a quartal harmonic construction, where chords are built by stacking fourths instead of thirds. We can hear the effect of this quartal chords in some guitar lines in songs by The Police (namely *Message in a Bottle*), in many King Crimson's and Robert Fripp's songs, in a large part of Fred Frith's production.

Melodic perfect fourth

The perfect fourth interval is wide enough to be felt like a jump, an assertive statement. This aspect is especially highlighted when the interval is placed in an ascending movement.

The most used example to illustrate the perfect fourth interval is Wagner's *Treulich Geführt*, the bridal chorale in the *Lohengrin*, which eventually became the standard wedding theme for any wedding. The melody starts with an ascending jump by a perfect fourth *F-Bb*, followed by a repetition of this *Bb* on a 'marching' rhythm. The ascending perfect fourth is the only relevant interval in this

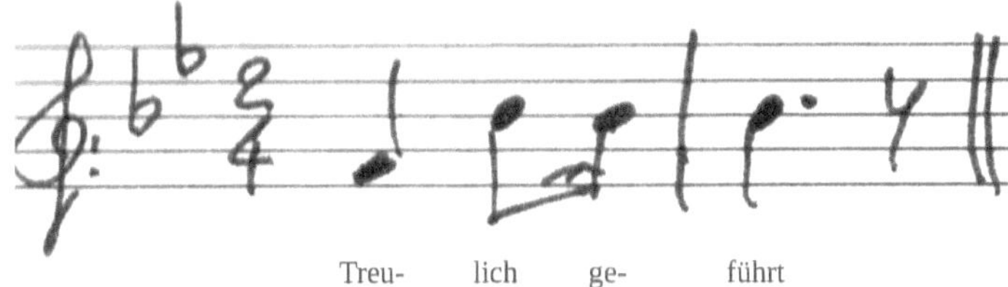

Fig. 47. Wagner, Treulich Geführt.

melodic phrase, where the other connotative element is the rhythmic movement, rather than the unisons. In that jump by a fourth we find the determination, the joy, the opening towards a prosperous future. It is a firm statement, that leaves no space for doubts.

In the *Marseillaise*, a song with a clear Jacobin matrix that eventually became the French national anthem, the perfect fourth appears between the third and the fourth note of the melody (the first three notes are repeated unisons on the typical rhythmic pattern of the Jacobin and revolutionary songs). Here, the tone of the ascending perfect fourth is epic, triumphant. The jump is wide enough to give us the idea of a proud walk, a large and self-confident gesture, though not so large to convey the idea of exaggeration, of a rage out of control, of a big distance or immense spaces: everything is on a human scale, a human that is confident, winning, determined.

I Want to Break Free by Queen presents another jump by an ascending perfect fourth at the beginning of the melody: *B-E* ("I want"). Then the melody rises again to the fifth and up to the major sixth. The whole movement of the melodic phrase conveys the image of breaking a border line, of going beyond, or at least of the desire to do so. The perfect fourth interval at the beginning plays a specific

Fig. 48. Marseillaise.

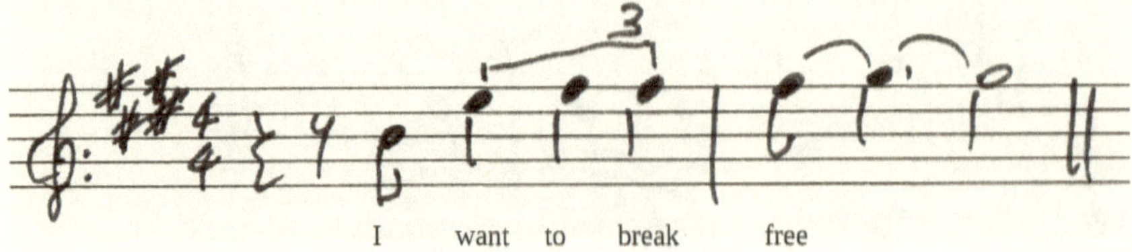

Fig. 49. Queen, I Want to Break Free.

role in this context: it gives us the idea of a strong statement that admits no discussions, a jump beyond the third of a chord arpeggio, a run-up to tear down a closed door.

The Beatles often use the perfect fourth interval in an ascending way. Let's see some examples. In *Back in the USSR* we find our interval at the end of the chorus, underlying that this is a determined statement, a foot put on the ground. The perfect fourth interval, first descending and then ascending, defines the beginning of the conclusive movement of the melody.

Fig. 50. The Beatles, Back in the USSR.

In *Birthday* the melody sung on the words "You say it's your birthday" starts with a jump by an ascending perfect fourth *E-A*, then goes up to an overall range of a minor sixth on a *C*. This kind of affirma-

Fig. 51. The Beatles, Birthday.

tive start with a perfect fourth interval is quite typical, and The Beatles use it quite often. One of its main characteristics is that the first note is at the end of a measure, so that the arrival point of this jump by a fourth falls on a strong beat, the first beat of the new measure. A similar situation is what we find in *Fixing a Hole*, with a jump by an ascending perfect fourth *C-F* at the beginning of the melody, again placed at the turn of the measures. Here, the rather bouncing rhythm and the insistence on the perfect fourth range both convey a playful and lively sense.

Fig. 52. The Beatles, Fixing a Hole.

In *I'll be There for You* by the Rembrandts, the theme from the famous tv show *Friends*, the perfect fourth interval plays a peculiar role. The first melodic phrase is sung over the lyrics "So no-one told you life was gonna be this way". The first two notes build an ascending perfect fourth interval *E-A*. Rather than a strong statement, this melodic gesture appears as the start of a speech in a rapid fashion, maybe even with a happy tone. After that, the melody keeps going up to an overall range of a minor seventh on *D*. From there, a first descending movement takes us down by a fourth, passing through all the intermediate degrees of the scale (*D-C#-B-A*). Then there is another jump by a descending perfect fourth *A-E* ("gonna"), and then again ascending to *A*, ending the phrase on the perfect fifth *B*. These

Fig. 53. Rembrandts, I'll be There for You.

Fig. 54. Elvis Presley, Love Me Tender.

repeated jumps and ranges by perfect fourths contribute to the happy and playful tone of the theme.

The melody in Elvis Presley's *Love Me Tender* starts as well with a jump by an ascending perfect fourth, dampened by a momentary descent on the major third (*D-G-F#-G*). Then the phrase ends with another jump by a perfect fourth, first descending and then ascending (*A-E-A*). The momentary passage on *F#* conveys a sense of tenderness, falling exactly on the word "tender". The rest of the melody, instead, uses assertive, almost exclamatory jumps by perfect fourths: "Love me tender, love me sweet".

Semantic field

The perfect fourth interval is usually considered as a consonant interval, though it might present a quite harsh character when it is not explicitly an inversion of the perfect fifth. In this case, it is perceived as undoubtedly concluding. The harshness of the interval is enhanced when it is used for harmonizations and when there is a movement by parallel fourth in the voices. On the other hand, it can be softened by a resolution, even a temporary one, on the third, especially on a major third, by just moving down a semitone.

The melodic movement by fourth is often used as an indicator of attack, a strong beginning of a speech. The open character of this melodic gesture can provoke associations with playful and joyful tones. In this sense, unlike the third intervals, the direction does not really change the semantic field of the interval.

Another very important association is with the sense of triumph, of proud marching, of an uncompromising decision: this association made it a particularly dear interval for anthems, marches and solemn occasions.

As an exercise, try to substitute the second note in *I'll be There for You* with a *G* or a *G#*. Listen how the open statement of the fourth interval is different from the uncertainty of a minor third or from the flirty and singsong attitude of the major third. Try also to substitute the perfect fourth interval on the word "gonna", for example with a smaller interval, or try to change the direction of the fourth upwards. In *I Want to Break Free*, try to substitute the second note with a unison, or with a jump by an octave. Since our ear is well trained in adjusting the variations from the known form, a brave attempt would be to try and change the perfect fourth intervals in the wedding march or in the *Marseillaise*. Try using very different intervals, like a minor third or a major second.

Chapter 6
The fifths

Harmonic diminished fifth

The diminished fifth interval covers three tones, that is six semitones. It is located exactly halfway in the distance between a note and its higher or lower octave. For this reason, an important feature of this interval is that its inversion is always the same: a diminished fifth.

It is a dissonant interval, maybe the dissonance par excellence, with a strong tension to resolve, usually moving by a semitone one or both the notes (preferably by countermovement). We can find it in many chords, hidden in not very prominent positions: for instance between the major third and the minor seventh in a major chord with an added minor seventh (in the *C7* chord, *C-E-G-Bb*, we find it between *E* and *Bb*). Or we can find it on the chord built on the VII degree of a major key, starting from the so called *leading note*, between the tonic note of the chord and its fifth. In the key of *C major*, the triad built on *B* will be made of the notes *B-D-F*. Between *B* and *F* there is a diminished fifth. In this case, its tendency to resolve the tension on the tonic, on the chord on the I degree (*C major*) that is just one semitone away, is particularly strong. Here, we can find a

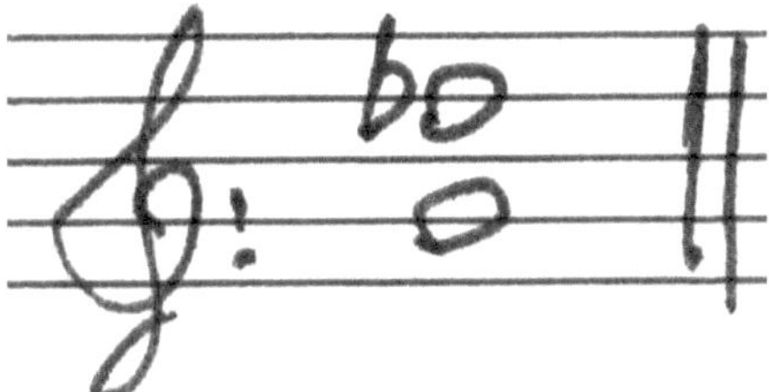

Fig. 55. The harmonic diminished fifth interval G-Db.

double resolution, with the tonic of the chord *B* going up a semitone to *C*, and *F* resolving down a semitone to *E*, that is the major third in the *C major* chord. In this kind of harmonic passage, the counter-movement of the voices contributes to convey a sense of pleasant conclusion of a harmonic sequence.

This three tones interval is also called *tritone*, and it is often associated with the idea of the 'diabolus in musica' (the devil in music). At the beginning of the 20th century, it was commonly thought that this interval was banned in the ancient musical practice, to the extent that it was considered as the devil transposed into music. This idea was exploited by many composers, who started using the tritone where dealing with themes connected to the underworld, to witchcraft, to supernatural, especially when it had evil connotations. The same principle was then recovered in rock music, especially by metal bands, who often associated it with the demonic and made a trademark of the use of it. Actually, it seems that the first text where we find the expression 'diabolus in musica' is from 1725, while the ancient musical essays addressed the tritone just as an unpleasant interval to be avoided. Sometimes they even invented musical systems organised in a way that avoided the presence of the tritone. Moreover, looking at the church music from the Medieval times, we can find many examples of tritones included in several passages, by the way without any reference to demons. In the *ars nova*, developed in the 14th century from the Notre Dame school, tritone passages are even considered as very refined virtuosos and musical embellishments: see specifically the works by Guillaume de Machaut, also his music for the church.

Melodic diminished fifth

In the melody of *The Simpsons'* theme song, written by Danny Elfman, the vocal line immediately goes up with a jump by a diminished fifth, then leaning on the perfect fifth ("The Simpsons"). The melodic phrase suggests a presentation in grand style, ruined by that stop on the diminished fifth, a semitone under the more glorious jump by a perfect fifth. It is like an unsuccessful jump, a stumbling when you are entering the scene. The sense of an incomplete fifth is obviously enhanced by the immediate adjustment on the perfect fifth.

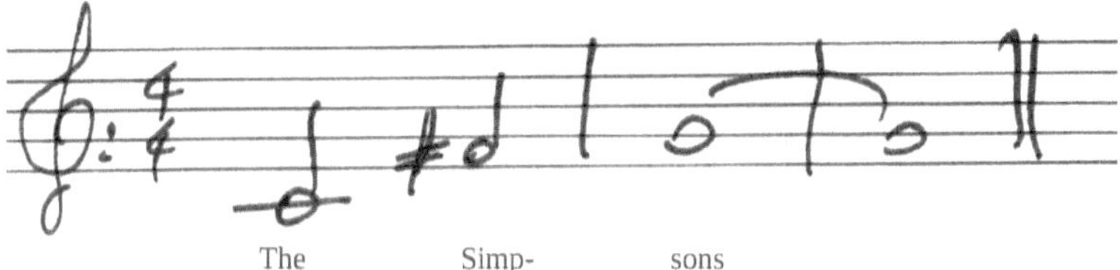

Fig. 56. The Simpsons, *by Danny Elfman.*

This diminished fifth interval also immediately defines that we are presenting a weird and eccentric family, with stories that use the absurd as a basis for irony.

The melodic diminished fifth interval is often used to create tension within a riff. *Purple Haze* by Jimi Hendrix starts with alternating chords that are a diminished fifth from each other. These chords give us a sense of great tension, amplifying the payoff of the resolution when the verse's harmonic sequence starts. The starting riff in *YYZ* by Rush is another emblematic example of the tension created by the diminished fifth interval, in this case in a descending version.

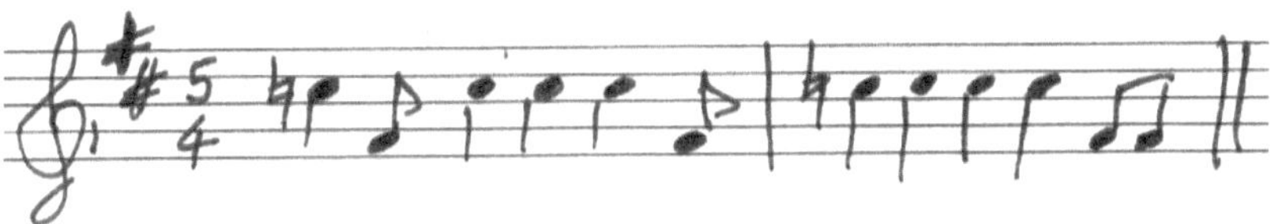

Fig. 57. Rush, YYZ.

The vocal melody in *Even Flow* by Pearl Jam starts with a strong descent by a diminished fifth on long notes *F#-C* ("Freezing"). The same movement returns at every new verse, highlighting the sinister, somehow distorted sense of the concept. Then, when the chorus

Fig. 58. Pearl Jam, Even Flow: *incipit of verse and chorus.*

Fig. 59. *Black Sabbath*, Black Sabbath.

comes ("Even flow"), the sensation of fluidity created by the new consonant interval is enhanced by the contrast with the initial tritone of the verse's melodic phrases.

Black Sabbath's *Black Sabbath* is another classical example of diminished fifth. The electric guitar starts the song with a series of sinister tritone intervals. And another important diminished fifth interval is placed in the vocal melodic line, at the end of the sentence "What is this that stands before me?". These last two words "before me" are sung on a passage from a high *G* to a passing *D* leading to that sinister *C#*, which is also a note outside the scale. Its position at the end of a melodic fragment that starts from the highest note of the whole phrase contributes to give special relevance to this demonic interval.

The main theme in *Peel the Paint* by Gentle Giant starts after the first two verses, when the lyrics say "Peel the paint". From then it goes on up to the end of the song, only interrupted with very rich passages and variations, in the characteristic style of the band. The riff is built on diminished fifth intervals: *G-C#-G-C / C-F#-C-F / F-B-F-Bb*, to conlcude with a wide scale. The riffs are played in unison by all the instruments, and also the vocal line follows them, interval after interval. While the instruments play the second series (*C-F#-C-F*) on a lower register, though, the voice goes up an octave in that moment. Here the tritone conveys in a masterful way the sense of frustration and sinister rage that permeates the whole lyrics: just think of the verse "Glass reflects what you are, it shows the face, the evil face of sin".

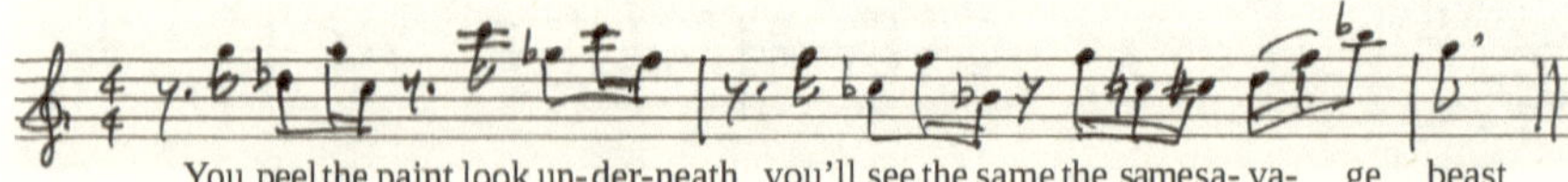

Fig. 60. *Gentle Giant*, Peel the Paint.

Semantic field

The diminished fifth interval is for several reasons the king of the dissonances. Its strong tension to resolve with a movement by semitone is its main feature. Its position exactly in the middle of the spectrum of intervals in the range of an octave makes its inversion identical to the original interval. Consequently, there is no substantial difference between an ascending and a descending diminished fifth. At the most, the direction of the interval can colour its sinister sense with a more open nuance when it is ascending, and a more closed shade when it is descending. In a text from 1555, *L'antica musica ridotta alla moderna prattica* (*Ancient Music Transferred to the Modern Practice*), Nicola Vincentino defines the tritone as 'lively and powerful' when it is ascending, 'funereal and sad' when it is descending. Nowadays, we often perceive it as sinister, but the lively aspect of its ascending version should not be underrated. The association of the tritone with the 'diabolus in musica' is often very clear in the use of the interval, though the historical accuracy of this association seems to be dubious. Musicologist Adam Neely made a very instructive video on the subject on Youtube (*The Great Myth of the Medieval Tritone Ban*, www.youtube.com/watch?v=3MhwGnq4N9o). Anyway, as a general rule, it has often been used to convey a sense of magic, witchcraft, demonic, sinister. The sense of tension is also a result of the incompleteness of the interval as compared to the perfect fifth. In this perspective, it has been also used as an incomplete, unsuccessful jump, a stumbling. Similarly, in a metaphorical sense, it can be associated to the threatening paranoia, or to an eccentric behaviour.

Try to substitute the second note in *The Simpsons'* theme song with a perfect fifth, repeated on the third note. It should be clear that it is our diminished fifth that gives that musical phrase all its character.

In *Even Flow* as well we can verify its relevance by substituting it for example with a unison: much of the tension would immediately disappear and the sense of the melody and of the whole song would be weakened.

Harmonic perfect fifth

The perfect fifth interval covers a distance of three tones and a half, or seven semitones from the starting note. Though it is just a semitone away from the interval that we defined as the king of the dissonances, the perfect fifth is one of the most consonant intervals of all. In the series of harmonics, or overtones, that make up a sound, the note at a distance of a fifth is the first to appear again and again, with a greater intensity than the higher overtones. This means that somehow it is already part of the starting note, therefore it can not be other than extremely consonant with it.

The perfect fifth is one of the three notes that make up a triad chord, both major and minor. From a harmonic point of view, this strong sense of stability makes it less suitable for a parallel movement in the voices: two voices or instruments playing parallel perfect fifth intervals would create an uninteresting movement, lacking tension. On the other hand, this is exactly what we find in the trumpet calls or in the attack signals of the horns.

The perfect fifth is also the inversion of a perfect fourth. Though we more frequently perceive the fourth as an inverted fifth, it is clear that the senses conveyed by these two intervals share many connotations.

Going further on semitone by semitone, the next interval after the perfect fifth would be the augmented fifth (four tones, or eight semitones). Again, we have an enharmonic interval with the minor sixth. Therefore, we are not talking here about the augmented fifth, choosing to call this interval minor sixth, as it is the most common use and since the sixth has a stronger sense, as we will see soon. From a harmonic point of view, though, there is one case that is worth mentioning: the augmented chord. Usually built stacking two major thirds over each other (for instance *C-E-G#*), the augmented chord is very

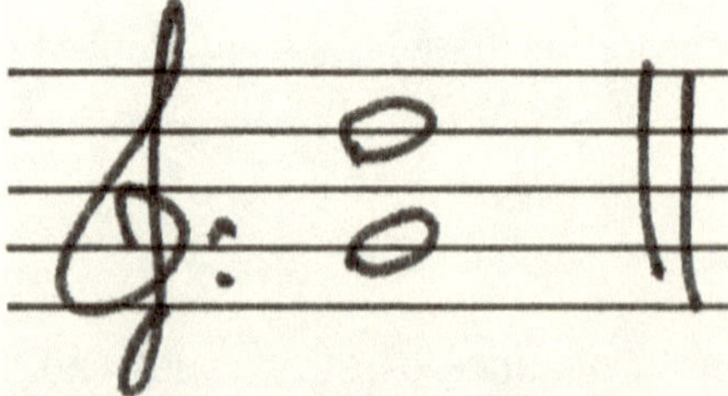

Fig. 61. The harmonic perfect fifth interval G-D.

unstable. It needs resolution. Substantially, it introduces an alternative harmonic dissonance to that of the dominant functions of the V and VII degrees, inserting a note that is not part of the scale, which tends to resolve to the higher next semitone, often only in the inner parts movement. Sometimes, the augmented chord is associated with the idea of the outer space: we find it often in themes from soundtracks for sci-fi movies and series.

Melodic perfect fifth

One of the most immediate examples that comes to mind when we think of a perfect fifth interval is the main theme from the soundtrack for *Star Wars*, written by John Williams. The melody starts with a jump by an ascending perfect fifth, that is rich of an epic and triumphant sense, but also recalls open spaces. It is such a connotating interval in the whole theme, that it is virtually impossible to substitute it with any other interval without drastically altering the sense conveyed by the melody. Moreover, since it is an exclusively instrumental theme, the attention dedicated to intervals, to the range of the melodic phrases and most of all to the beginning of the themes is particularly important.

Still in the context of the soundtracks for films, the theme song of *The Flintstones* starts with a descending jump by a perfect fifth. It is a firm and precise statement, without hesitation, almost an exclamation mark, enhanced in this sense by the break that follows the second note.

In *Blackbird* by The Beatles, the melody starts with a series of short and agitated notes in unison, concluding the phrase with an ascending jump by a perfect fifth *G-D*, corresponding to the longest

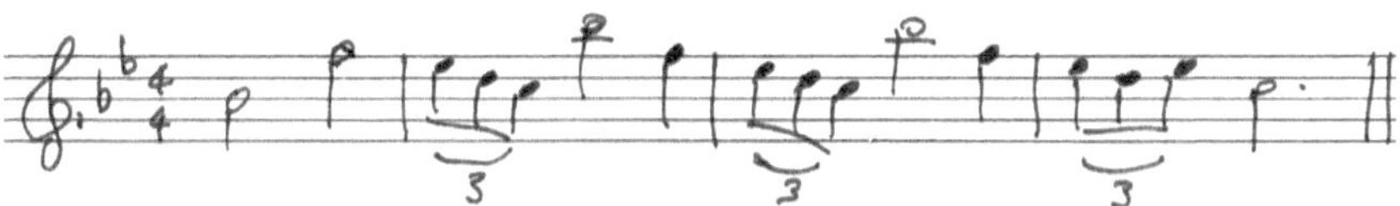

Fig. 62. Star Wars Theme, *by John Williams.*

Fig. 63. Meet the Flintstones.

notes: the last two notes on the sentence "Blackbird singing in the dead of night". Here, the idea is both conclusive, as a strong and wide ending of the phrase – that up to this moment just stayed on the very same note – and opening, preparing the next phrases, which articulate the muscal discourse. None of them will ever reach the height of the conclusive *D* in the first phrase, and none of them will reach notes below the initial *G*. That interval at the end of the first phrase defines in a single jump the melodic range of the whole musical passage.

Fig. 64. The Beatles, Blackbird.

In *My Favourite Things,* written by Richard Rodgers for the musical *The Sound of Music,* the melody is strongly characterized by

Fig. 65. My Favourite Things, *by Richard Rodgers.*

Fig. 66. Simple Minds, Don't You Forget About Me.

the ascending perfect fifth in the first notes *E-B-B* ("Raindrops on"). Then the melody proceeds going even lower than the starting *E*, to be precise reaching a *B* a perfect fourth below. Remember that fourth and fifth are somehow specular intervals, since they are reciprocal inversions. Here the jump suggests happiness: in the end we are making a list of our 'favourite things', the things that make us happy. And the repetition of the melodic phrase highlights exactly this character of a list.

The melody in *Don't You Forget About Me* by Simple Minds is strongly affected by the descending perfect fifth interval *C-F*, coming back at the beginning of each melodic phrase. All the variations occur in the following section of the phrase, while our interval is a constant that always comes back, a sort of anchorage. So much that it comes back in the chorus' melody as well. The jump by a perfect fifth is quite wide and assertive, though the descending movement softens a little the exclamative effect.

Another example of descending movement by a perfect fifth is provided by *Feelings* by Morris Albert. Here, the descent from *B* to *E* is followed by a long pause, a clear break that highlights even more the interval. In this case, we can see even more clearly how the descending movement enhances an almost melancholic aspect of the perfect fifth. Partly, this is due to the proximity of the minor sixth (just a semitone away) and therefore to the strong semantic field connected to the sixth (see next chapter). Gino Stefani, for example in

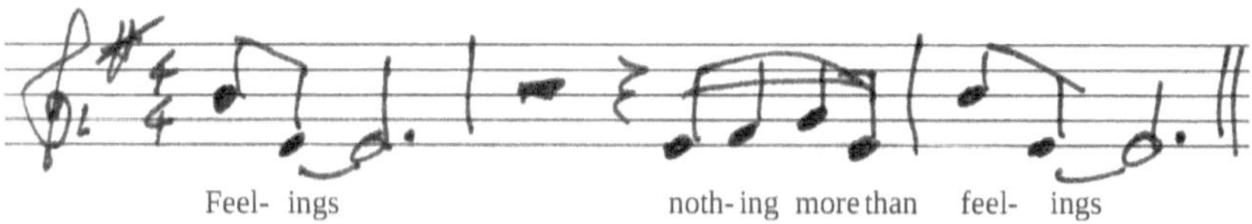

Fig. 67. Morris Albert, Feelings.

La competenza musicale (*Musical Competence*), analised the ability of the perfect fifth to assume a certain taste of 'past'. So we might say, by extension, a taste of sentiments related to the past, like melancholy.

Another example where the solid perfect fifth interval is strongly affected by the proximity of the sixth is *Love of My Life* by Queen. Here the melody starts with a descending minor second interval *C-B*, then coming back to *C* and jumping by an ascending fifth to *G* ("Love of my life"). The *B* on the second note essentially stretches the range of the melodic phrase to a minor sixth, certainly a sweeter interval compared to the fifth. So, when our interval appears, though it is ascending, we perceive the openness and width of the perfect fifth, but also a nuance of tenderness from the sixth.

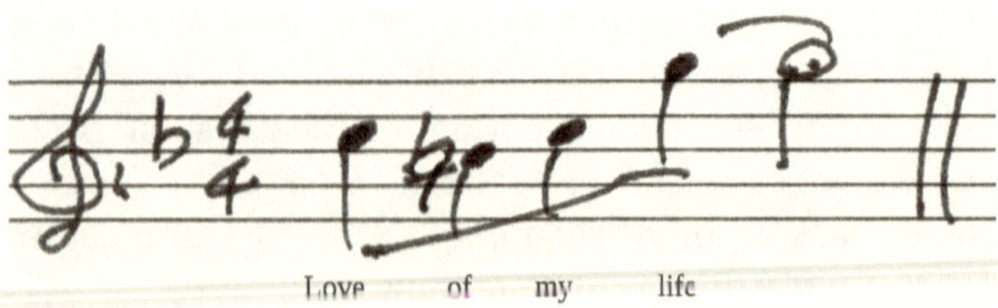

Fig. 68. Queen, Love of My Life.

Semantic field

The perfect fifth interval, as the fourth, corresponds to a starting signal, an attack, but also to a conclusion or a statement. Since it is wider than the fourth, it has a stronger character of openness and exclamation. It is a quite wide and vigorous jump to a consonant, stable note. It is a wide, open, confident and assertive gesture. Even in its descending version, it keeps a strong sense of statement. Its proximity with the powerful sense of the sixth can colour the perfect fifth with a melancholic taste, especially when it is descending or when a passage in the melody defines an overall melodic range of a sixth.

As for the two soundtrack themes, it is easy to understand that it is not possible to substitute the starting perfect fifth. We can try anyway, to verify more precisely the sense conveyed by that attack. Let's try instead to substitute the perfect fifth interval in *Blackbird*. What happens if we used an *A* and a *G* instead of ending on the *D* repeated twice? All of a sudden it seems as if we had a completely different song in front of us!

In *My Favourite Things*, the perfect fifth interval is used on lyrics that list, indeed, the favourite things. Let's try to substitute it with a major third interval, that, as we saw, can easily be suitable for a list. The result is more singsong and less wide: we feel a little less the joy that these things can bring us. We know that the fourth and the fifth intervals are quite similar. But are they interchangeable? Let's try to substitute these fifths with fourths to see what nuances make the fifth the most suitable interval in this case.

In *Feelings* we saw how the gravitational influence of the semantic field of the sixth can affect a descending perfect fifth interval, if the context is adequately processed. Let's try to substitute this interval with a descending perfect fourth *B-F#*. I would also like to stress once again that no interval in music stands on its own, isolated from a context. Context is important, it is crucial: the chords, the harmonic sequence, the movement of the other parts, the rhythm, the fullness and emptiness and so on. Here, we are trying to isolate the phenomenon interval in order to analyse it in its essence, but no musical analysis should ever forget to take the context into consideration.

Chapter 7
The sixths

Harmonic minor sixth

The minor sixth interval covers a distance of four tones, that is eight semitones, between two notes. It is an enharmonic interval with the augmented fifth, but it is commonly called minor sixth, except when it is included in the augmented chords as we mentioned in the previous chapter.

From a harmonic point of view, the minor sixth can be considered as a major third inversion. In this case, since the major third is a consonant interval, also the sixth keeps a consonant role within the chord. Its tension towards the very close perfect fifth, though, can be exploited to create a strong connection in a harmonic sequence, creating a resolution of a tension with a movement by a semitone.

There is also a peculiar case: the so called 'Neapolitan sixth' chord. Its name is a bit misleading, since it is based on a correspondence with the notes of the so called 'neapolitan' scale, which has little to do with the local folk tradition, but shares some typical intervals with it. This way of overlaying voices was very popular in the Baroque era, before the invention of tonal harmony. But since it creates a strong tension and involves an exotic character, it found a

Fig. 69. The harmonic minor sixth interval G-Eb.

place in the theory and practice of the 18th and 19th centuries as well. We can find examples of Neapolitan sixths also in Beethoven. It is essentially a chord built on the IV degree of the scale, therefore a sort of parallel subdominant function. This chord, though, is minor and, instead of the fifth, includes the minor sixth: for instance *F-Ab-Db* in the key of *C major* or *C minor*. In this case we won't consider it as an augmented fifth. First of all because the scale implies a note on the perfect fifth spot, *C* in our example, since that is the tonic of the whole key. Secondly, because the augmented chords typically involve a major third, while here we have a minor third (in our example, *F-Ab*). Now, we could undoubdtedly consider this triad as a *Db major (Db-F-Ab)* chord inversion, returning to the usual stacking of alternating thirds. Still, we need to keep in mind that this particular harmonic configuration always appears only with the IV degree on bass (*F* in our example). Usually, this chord is used in place of the subdominant on the IV degree, to get to the dominant chord on the V degree, preparing the final and conclusive cadence on the I degree of the scale. This particular movement derives from the tension created by the minor sixth resolving usually by an ascending semitone, achieving the fifth of the V degree chord: in the key of *C major*, the sixth note *Db* goes up to *D*, which is the fifth in the chord *G-B-D*, that is the V degree and dominant chord of the key. In the meantime, the third of the Neapolitan chord descends by a semitone, landing on the tonic note of the V degree chord: in the key of *C major*, the third note of the chord, *Ab*, goes down to *G*, which is the tonic note in the chord *G-B-D*, the dominant chord in the key of *C major*. An alternative movement of the voices could rely on the cromatic tension (by semitones) of the Neapolitan sixth chord, creating a directional movement by semitones within a voice's line, often the bass. In fact, the Neapolitan sixth chord already includes notes which are alien to the key: in a minor key, it adds the lowered second degree (in the key of *C minor*, we should not find the note *Db*, since it should be *D*); in a major key, it also adds the lowered sixth degree (in the key of *C major*, we should not find neither the *Db* nor the *Ab*). These temporarily altered notes can be interpreted and used to create a cromatic passage, moving the voices in a way that creates even more intriguing harmonic sequences.

Another peculiar case, somehow connected to the chord we just described, comes from the harmonic, or melodic, minor scale modes: essentially scales where the seventh degree is altered (harmonic minor scale), or the seventh and sixth degree as well are altered (melodic minor scale), by raising them by a semitone to respond to the harmonic requirements for the chord generated from these scales. So, the *A* natural minor scale (*A-B-C-D-E-F-G-A*) will change into *A-B-C-D-E-F-G#-A* for the harmonic scale and *A-B-C-D-E-F#-G#-A* for the melodic scale. Using this new set of notes, if we build a scale starting from the fifth note *E*, we get a scale that includes a major third and a minor sixth as well. A very peculiar case, which can cause tensions towards the fifth degree of the scale, or harmonic overlayings of the voices that resemble the Neapolitan sixth quite a lot.

Melodic minor sixth

The melodic minor sixth interval is charged with a very strong sense, so strong that it can affect the other intervals in the melodic phrase, tingeing them, partly at least, with its colours, even if it appears only as an overall range of the melody, rather than a proper interval.

The theme from the soundtrack of the 1970 movie *Love Story*, written by Francis Lai and recorded later by Andy Williams, with lyrics by Carl Sigman and a new title *Where Do I Begin?*, is almost entirely built on a descending minor sixth interval *Bb-D*, followed then by an ascending sixth *C-A*. The tone of tenderness and sweetness of the melody is entirely contained in these intervals, so much that the lack of other notes makes the melody almost cheesy. Gino Stefani defines the sixth as the 'interval of the heart, the melodic interval par excellence'. This song is a perfect exemplification of both these aspects. The differences in the sense of a minor and a major sixth are

Fig. 70. Where Do I Begin?, *by Francis Lai and Carl Sigman.*

no more relevant when we are confronted with the great impact of the jump between two notes separated by eight or nine semitones. In this melody, we find both intervals, minor and major sixth, close enough to each other to allow us to compare them. In the first case, the see-saw between the notes starts from a jump by a descending minor sixth: as we already should have understood, the downward direction is often associated to melancholy, sadness, closure, resignation. The second interval, the major sixth, on the other hand, is initially placed on an ascending jump, therefore it is a little wider and more assertive, but still clearly a sixth.

In Scott Joplin's *The Entertainer* we find another ascending minor sixth *E-C* in the second measure, starting from the third note of the melody. This interval is repeated three times in a row, before letting the melody develop towards the conclusion of the phrase. Here, the ascending direction of the sixth affects the sense, keeping the strong melodic character of the interval, while softening its sweetness and tenderness aspects. The immediate repetition of the interval contributes in conveying this sense of melodiousness rather than sentimentalism. What remains is a quite wide jump upwards, which does not aim at another note, but instead it is meaningful on its own, and repeated to assert itself as a reference unit, compared to which the rest of the melody must widen to define its happy and bouncing character.

In *Johanna*, a song included in the 1979 musical *Sweeny Todd*, eventually adapted by Tim Burton in 2007 for the screen, we immediately find an ascending jump by a minor sixth *G-Eb* ("I feel you"). This correspondence of the interval with the expression of a feeling in the lyrics is all but an accident. The minor sixth expresses all the sentimentalism of the words. The ascending direction contributes to tinge with hope the character's expression. The end of the phrase goes down by a semitone, resolving the tension on the perfect fifth

Fig. 71. The Entertainer, *by Scott Joplin.*

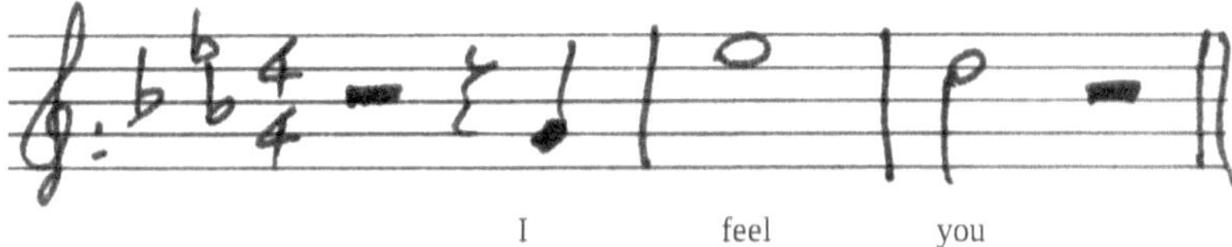

Fig. 72a. Johanna, *by Stephen Sondheim: beginning.*

interval, in relation to the first *G* of the melody. After this beginning with long notes, the melody becomes faster, with tighter intervals, until two moments that are interesting from our point of view for the analysis of intervals. The sentence "Satisfied enough to dream you"is matched with a diminished fifth interval *C-Gb* that falls on the word "dream", coming out of the blue, like a thunderbolt in a clear sky, tingeing that dream with a sinister premonition. In the next melodic phrase ("Happily I was mistaken"), we find a minor seventh interval *C-Bb* exactly on the word "mistaken". As we will see in the next chapter, one of the possible semantic fields of the seventh is a wide but incomplete jump, a miscalculation, as in the verse that the character is singing, which in fact reaches then the note a tone higher, the octave, as if to adjust that false step.

In The Beatles repertoire as well we find examples of minor sixths. In *She's a Woman*'s first verse, "My love don't give me presents", our interval *C#-a* falls exactly on the words "my love", highlighting the association of the sixth with the sense of love, heart, feeling. Should we substitute this interval with a more threatening one, like a diminished fifth or a seventh, the whole sentence would take a different meaning, turning maybe into an accusation or some sort of doubt regarding a woman who never gives us presents! In *My Life*, we find instead the ascending minor sixth *E-C* in the second melodic phrase. The lyrics go: "There are places I'll remember all

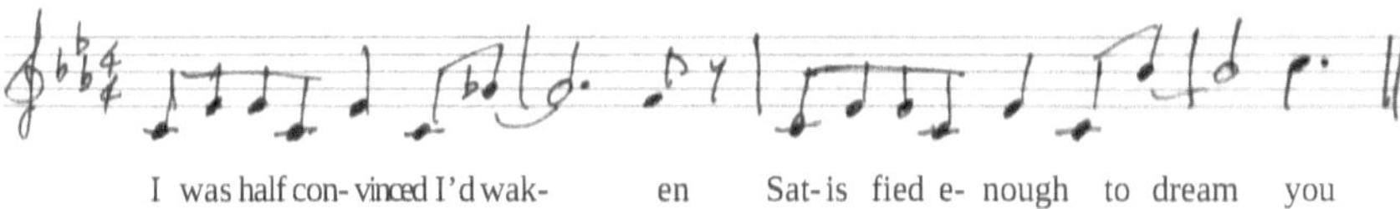

Fig. 72b. Johanna, *by Stephen Sondheim: extract from the melody.*

Fig. 73. The Beatles, She's a Woman.

my life, though some have changed". Our interval falls on the words "some have changed", as if to stress the emotional effect of these changes. In the second verse, the same interval falls on the words "I still recall", giving a melancholic sense to this memory.

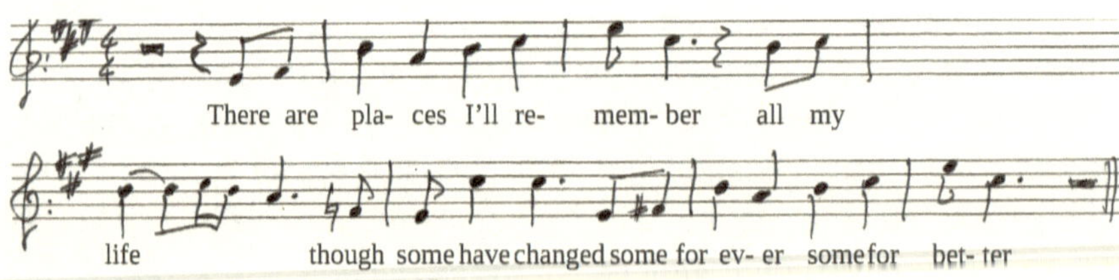

Fig. 74. The Beatles, In My Life.

Seasong by Robert Wyatt presents one of the most complex and intriguing melodies in pop and rock music. The melodic discourse builds a very long arch before finding its conclusion, stopping on quite inventing notes, in an intricate journey, with wide intervals and an extremely wide overall range. The whole melodic phrase is strongly connoted by the initial ascending jump by a minor sixth E-

Fig. 75. Robert Wyatt, Seasong.

C: "You look different". The phrase then leans on the fourth (*A*: "every time"), jumps to the octave and descends by semitones to the minor seventh *D* ("you come"). The stopping points feel uncertain, almost never on really conclusive intervals, until the end of the long melodic phrase, conferring a dreaming atmosphere to the song. The ascending minor sixth interval used at the beginning of the phrase strongly affects the sense of the whole melody, immediately plunging us into a melancholic and intimate atmosphere, though the melody shows a wide range rather than intimate and a number of jumps rather than a melancholic scalar movement.

Nothing Compares 2 U is a song by Prince, though it gained a lot in the version by Sinead O' Connor. The atmosphere is sad, intimate, melancholic, sentimental, especially in Sinead O' Connor's cover. Yet, the first proper sixth in the melody only comes on the second chorus ("'cause nothing compares, nothing compares to you"). The second "nothing" is varied with an ascending jump by a minor sixth *A-F*, immediately redescending to *A*. The very high register enhances the tormented sense conveyed by the interval.

Fig. 76. Sinead O' Connor, Nothing Compares 2 U, *written by Prince.*

Semantic field

The sixth interval, in Gino Stefani's words, is 'the interval of the heart, the most melodic of all intervals'. It is usually associated with love, sweetness, tenderness, sentiment, but also melancholy and sadness for something lost. Specifically, the minor sixth is more associated to grief and melancholy, as compared to the major sixth, especially but not exclusively when its movement is descending. It is the interval of the heart, often used even in a sneaky way, for instance in advertisements to associate a product with a sensation of tenderness and sensuality. Among all the intervals, this is the most melodic: wide though not excessive, pleasant, tender, moving and satisfying. Moreover, unlike the fourth or the fifth, it has no harmonic function, showing a distinctly melodic nature and stretching its semantic field to symbolically embrace even flight and dream. It has such a strong impact that it is decisive even just as an overall range of the melody, or when it appears only in a second moment. This is the case, for instance, of *Nothing Compares 2 U*, where it only shows up in the second chorus, but once it is established in our memory of that song, it resounds in the atmosphere since the beginnig of the piece. It is also the case of *Feelings*, where the main interval is the perfect fifth in the verse, but when the chorus comes in, the notes get longer, the melody flies and the word "feelings" falls on an interval stretched up to a minor sixth. As soon as the sixth interval appears, we clearly perceive that the song is sad and we transfer this interpretation to the previous fifths as well. It should be said, by the way, that the way the singer interprets the melody has its relevance here, since he 'glides' the perfect fifth of the verse in a way that is already somehow melancholic, thus guiding our perception of the interval.

In the folk tradition, we find plenty of sixth intervals, especially minor. Specifically, it is used in a very expressive way, for instance, in the anarchists songs, where a sense of fraternity in the truth and humanity is produced by the interval of the heart.

In the melody of the theme of *Love Story*, the minor sixth interval is particularly relevant. Try to sing the verse "Where do I begin" as a step by step descent covering a range of a fourth: the whole song now has a completely different sense.

Try now to substitute the three consecutive sixths of *The Entertainer* with a different interval, for instance a fourth, or a major third. Even when there is no lyrics guiding our interpretation of the musical sense, the intervals, especially the sixth, tell us a precise story, forging a certain atmosphere in such an accurate way that even words could not achieve.

If we don't put the sixth interval in *Nothing Compares 2 U*, the risk is that the whole melody of the song becomes more monotonous, less expressive, almost as if a big part of the expressive and evocative strenght of the songs relied on that single note.

Harmonic major sixth

The major sixth interval covers a distance of four tones and a half, that is nine semitones. As for the minor sixth, from a harmonic point of view it is prevalently considered as an inversion of the minor third, which is part of the triad of a minor chord.

The major sixth can be added to a triad to get the sixth chord. In both major and minor chords, the added sixth is alway a major sixth: *C-E-G-A* for a *C major* chord; *C-Eb-G-A* for a *C minor* chord. Adding a sixth produces somehow a sense of harmonic uncertainty. If we take a major triad and add a sixth, we get a set of notes that can be reorganised in a different order as a minor chord with the added seventh, whose harmonic function is easier to interpret: for example *A-C-E-G*. The notes are exactly the same as those of the major chord with an added sixth and, as we know from the examples with the inversions, a chord is never defined by the order of the notes. On the other hand, the sixth is often added without a specific function, as a colour added to the chord, just like in Debussy's expressionists dictates.

As for the scales that can go with the chords, the minor scale built on the second degree of a given major key (for instance starting from *D* in the key of *C major*) always includes a major sixth (*D-B*): *D-E-F-G-A-B-C-D*. This scale is called dorian. Its character is defined by the major sixth, which differentiates it from all the other scales or modes in that key. It is also the only minor scale within the tonality that includes a major sixth instead of a minor sixth. The dorian mode is by far the most used for solos. It became a sort of a standard after being the starting reference for so many jazz improvisations on wind instruments (trumpet, saxophone and so on).

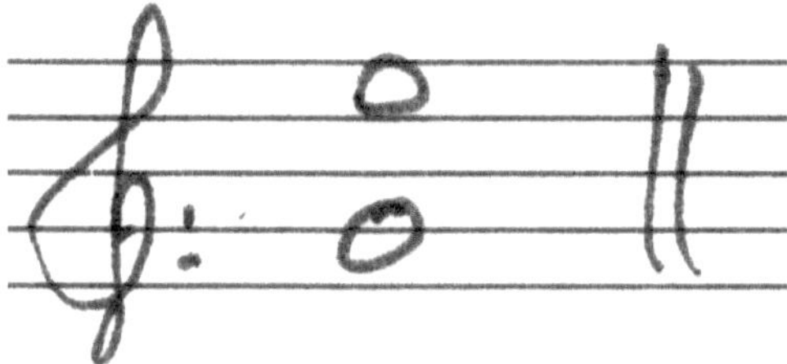

Fig. 77. The harmonic major sixth interval G-E.

Melodic major sixth

In *Princess Leia's Theme*, a tune included in the *Star Wars* soundtrack, we find an ascending major sixth *A-F#* at the beginning of the melody, followed by an ascending movement by semitone to the minor seventh *G* and then a suspended rest on the perfect fifth *E*. So, we have an immediate 'jump of the heart', a very melodious leap that connotes the theme that corresponds to the character of princess Leia. The rest of the melodic phrase dances around the note of this sixth interval, then resting on the fifth and remaning a little suspended. Therefore, the major sixth interval is without any doubt the most connotative interval in the melodic phrase, creating very precise associations with the character it represents, though it is not so easy to explain those associations with words.

Fig. 78. Princess Leia's Theme, *by John Williams.*

Another famous instrumental song that starts with a major sixth is Duke Ellington's *Take the A Train*. The first part of the melody is all centered around the ascending major sixth jump from *G* to *E* and then back down to *G*. The phrase ends with a descending interval *E-Ab*, shifting the range to a minor sixth: it is the same major sixth we heard at the beginning, but this time a little smaller. Here, the sixth major interval is used more in the sense of 'melodic par excellence', rather than a 'jump of the heart'. Being so large, it conveys the idea

Fig. 79. Duke Ellington, Take the A Train.

Fig. 80. My Way, *by Revauz e François.*

of a wide movement, yet a pleasant one, not an exclamation, almost just a wink.

In *My Way*, a song written by Jacques Revaux and Claude François – the English lyrics are an addition by Paul Anka – but made especially famous by Frank Sinatra's interpretation, we find another example of major sixth. The first three melodic phrases ("And now / The end is near / And so I face") all start with the same ascending jump from *G* to *E*. The main feature of the interval is its melodiousness here as well. But the insistence in the following two phrases starts to convey a sense of melancholy, that becomes explicit at the end of the verse with a descending minor second from *D* to *C#*. Then, the second verse opens with an ascending sixth jump transferred on the next higher tone ("My friend"). This time, though, it is a minor sixth, that gives even more sense of melancholy and resignation to the whole melody. Even in the irriverent version made by Sex Pistols of this song, despite the purposely incertain intonation on the final notes, the sixth interval can be clearly identified. Maybe we might argue that in the Sex Pistols' version there is a little less a resigned tone and more angry melancholy, deluded by the lack of sense of everythimg in life.

A particularly effective example of ascending major sixth is included in *America, the Beautiful,* written by Katherine Lee Bates and very popular in the United States as a patriotic song (Elvis Presley used to perform it often during his concerts). Here, the jump by a sixth falls on "America, America", and it comes not as a purely melodic gesture, but rather as a passionate patriotic call.

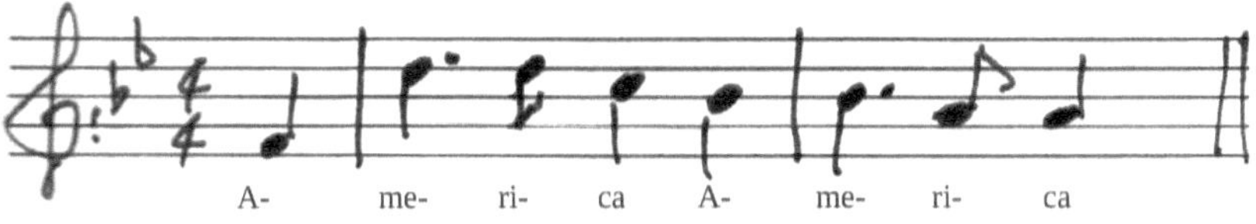

Fig. 81. America, the Beautiful, *by Katherine Lee Bates.*

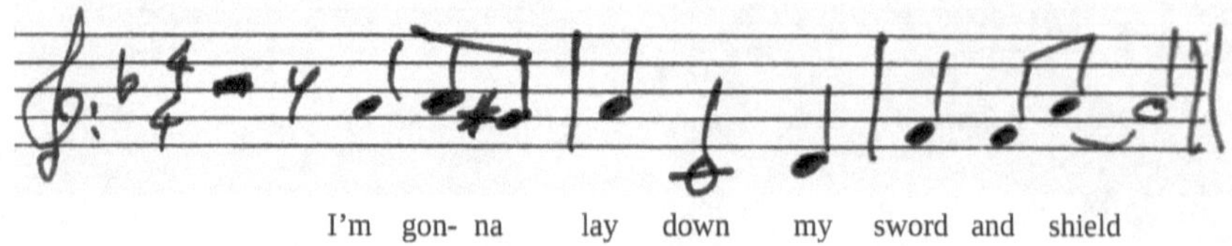

Fig. 82. Down By the Riverside.

We can find a lot of sixths in the blues and especially gospel tradition as well. An example is the traditional *Down By the Riverside*. I suggest listening to Louis Armstrong's and Pete Seger's versions, though there are many other interpretations. The first verse says: "I'm gonna lay down my sword and shield". Exactly on the words "lay down" we find a descending jump by a major sixth which, while following the sense of downward direction expressed in the lyrics, also colours this descent with a sense of suffering that no other interval could convey so well.

The last example I will quote is *Over the Rainbow*, written by Harold Arlen and originally sung by Judy Garland in the movie *The Wizard of Oz*. The melody starts with an ascending jump by an octave *F-F* ("Somewhere"), but then goes down from the major seventh to the perfect fifth and then up again to the octave, passing through the major sixth *D* (*E-C-D-E-F*). And in the second phrase ("way up high") our ascending major sixth *F-D* appears explicitly as a long notes interval, colouring with dream and melancholic desire that range of an octave that otherwise would sound exclamatory. It needs to be highlighted that already in the first phrase, just the only precence of the sixth, hidden in a melodic phrasing, is enough to define the atmosphere of the melody.

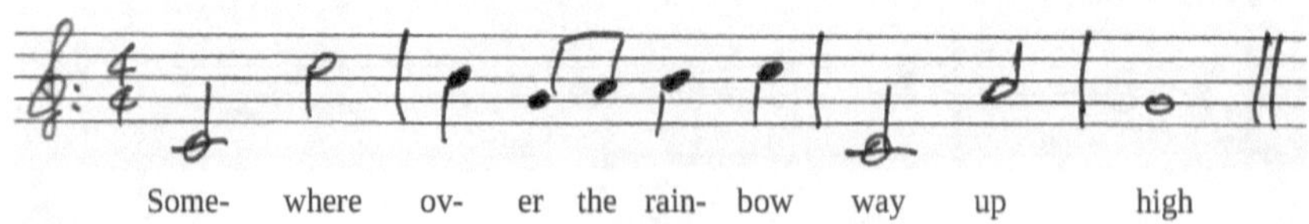

Fig. 83. Over the Rainbow, *by Harold Arlen.*

Semantic field

The major sixth interval maintains the same fundamental features as the minor sixth, though with a stronger association with the flight, the dream, the melodious singing. It is a wider interval, even if only for one semitone, therefore it conveys more the idea of a wide space, of a jump, of taking off. The connection between the sixth and the theme of flying appears evident in songs like *Over the Rainbow*, as well as in many soundtracks and classical compositions. When the sixth is minor, there is a touch of sadness, tenderness, melancholy. When the sixth is major, the interval is often associated with a patriotic sense, as in *America, the Beautiful*, or an euphoric sense, as in *La Traviata* by Verdi, where the sixth becomes the melodic gesture of the toast to the will to live. I will never stress enough the power of this interval, that is able to contaminate with its sense any other interval as well as whole melodic phrases, even when it is 'hidden' in a passage or just implied as a melodic range. Being able to identify it can also be a critical defense against those who use it as a subliminal message, for instance in advertisings.

Try to substitute the major sixth *E* in *Take the A Train* with a minor sixth *Eb*. Suddenly the atmosphere changes from joyful to more melancholic. Yet we can say that the general sense of the melody is not so far from the original.

Do the same thing with *America, the Beautiful*. Here, instead, the patriotic sense suffers a serious blow and the nostalgic tone becomes almost an accusation, a reproach. Surely a regret for what could have been, instead of a triumphant jump full of stars and stripes patriotism.

If we change the starting interval in *My Way*, maybe moving down the melody by a major second, the whole song acquires a completely different sense.

Try also to eliminate the leaning on *Bb* on the second note of the melody in *Love of My Life*, quoted in the previous chapter about the fifth, but with a range of sixth created exactly by that *Bb*. By taking the *Bb* away, thus reducing the range of the melody, the following jump by a perfect fifth gets a completely different feel.

Chapter 8
The sevenths

Harmonic minor seventh

The minor seventh interval covers a distance of five tones, or ten semitones. It is one of the largest intervals, strictly related to the octave, that is to the tonic note of the scale and of the key, to which it is very close.

From a harmonic point of view, it is a dissonant interval, but the extensive use in blues, jazz and rock music accumstomed our ear to perceive it as a mild dissonance. It has a double tension: on one hand it can resolve on the more reassuring major sixth, just a semitone down; on the other hand, it can tend to resolve going up a tone to the octave. The descending semitone resolution is usually hidden within the movements of the chord parts. Much more frequent is its tensive relation towards the octave, with reference also to the backdoor resolution of the blues, discussed earlier in chapter 3 on the major second. In fact, the minor seventh's inversion is exactly a major second.

In tertiary harmony, where the chords are built by stacking thirds over each other, the minor seventh appears as the higher third added to a basic triad in almost every minor chord and in one particular species of major chord. It is the chord built on the V degree of the key, the dominant chord. In the key of *C major*, for instance, we can

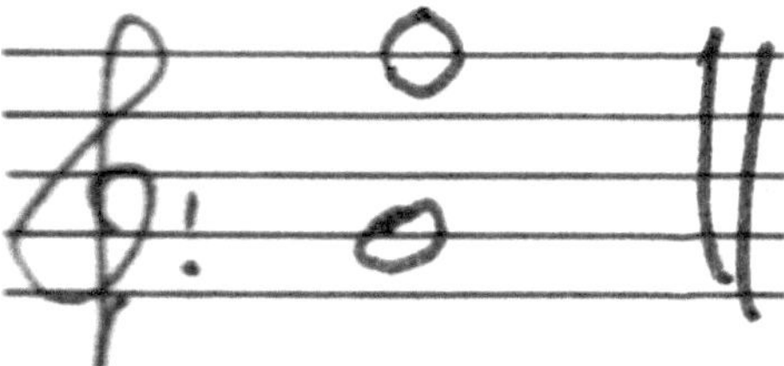

Fig. 83. The harmonic minor seventh interval G-F.

add a further (minor) third, that is a *F*, to the triad of *G major* (*G-B-D*). In the movement from the V to the I degree (from *G major* to *C major*), which is the so called authentic cadence – the basis of most of the harmonic movements and of the harmonic syntax in classical harmony – the note *F* often goes down a semitone to *E*, that is the third in the *C major* chord (*C-E-G*). This descending resolution is enhanced by the simultaneous ascending movement of *B* (the third in the *G major chord*) to *C*.

The dominant relationship between two chords separated by a fifth is so strong that it generates the possibility of secondary dominants. Essentially, any major chord can tend towards a chord that is a perfect fifth away in a dominant relationship. Using this principle in a sequence of chords all separated a fifth from each other, secondary dominants, we get the harmonic sequence called *turnaround*, often used in jazz and blues. Moreover, the position of the seventh as a natural addition in the pattern of stacking thirds to a basic triad makes it a natural choice to give a particular taste to the chord, despite its harmonic function. So, in most of the blues and blues-derived rock repertoire we find major chords with the minor seventh at every single harmonic change, without the need for a cadence or secondary dominant relationship.

Melodic minor seventh

The iconic melody of the opening tune of the tv series *Star Trek*, written by Alexander Courage, is strongly connoted by the minor seventh interval. After an introduction that is at the same time epic and misterious, connoted by wide intervals as well, including minor sevenths, the proper melody starts in a very recognisable manner with an ascending jump by a minor seventh *G-F*, before going gradually down and stopping on a *Bb* (minor third of *G*). The second melodic phrase starts with a very similar jump, this time an octave

Fig. 84. Star Trek Theme, *by Alexander Courage.*

G-G, while the following descent stops on *B* (major third of *G*). In the following parts, the melody includes cromatic passages and even major seventh passages, but here we will consider just the first two melodic phrases. The ascending minor seventh jump immediately conveys the idea of enormous spaces and epic adventures but, since it doesn't make it to the octave, the tone sounds more misterious and less glorious. The choice of the minor seventh, instead of a major seventh, avoids a too strong tension, which would convey a stronger sense of incompleteness and maybe also of danger. The parallel with the start of the second phrase – this time on an octave interval decisevely more complete – highlights the role of the minor seventh in the initial phrase. The final goal of the two phrases contrasts as well in a similar way: the first phrase, started with a misterious and incomplete jump, ends on the minor third in relation to the starting note, amplifying the sense of mystery even more; the second phrase, more epic and complete with its jump by an octave, ends instead on the major third, with a sense of conclusive destination, a happy ending. In these two melodic phrases and in the use of the intervals, we are already told about the whole epic of a journey to infinte and misterious spaces, with adventures filled with dangerous situations, heroic deeds and a happy ending.

The melody in *Somewhere*, written by Leonard Bernstein for the musical *West Side Story* in 1957, starts with a descending jump by a minor seventh *B-A*. Then, the melody leans downwards on *G#* and descends down to *C#* ("There's a place for us"). The starting jump corresponds to a large space, a leap of hope, maybe a bit excessive and therefore immediately adjusted with a descent by semitone to *G#*, a major sixth, the interval of the heart.

Watermelon Man is a famous jazz instrumental song by Herbie Hancock, first recorded in 1962. Though there are many versions of

Fig. 85. Somewhere, *by Leonard Bernstein.*

Fig. 86. Herbie Hancock, Watermelon Man.

this tune, I will refer here to that first recording, because I find it more useful for our goals. The melody starts with a descending minor seventh passage by the trumpet, from a long *Eb* to a conclusive phrase that begins with two repeated *F* and then goes up to *C*, to *D* and ends on *F*. The second melodic phrase is completely identical, but this time the starting note is a higher *F*, with a descending jump by an octave, as if to adjust the uncertainty of the first phrase. The result is sensual but also playful, in no way intimate, since the jump is too large to convey such a feeling.

In *Lady Jane* by Rolling Stones, we find a minor seventh jump, first descending and then ascending, on the second section of the melody, that we could identify as a refrain or maybe more precisely as the B melodic section in a form ABAB, typical of the music for dance and for the halls of the ancient courts (please refer to the third book of this series *Musical Structures* for a deeper analysis of the musical forms). The song has an Elizabethan tone, explicitly in the use of dulcimer and in the Chaucerian English used in the lyrics. But while in the opening melody these are the only two factors that recall the Elizabethan court halls, in the second section the musical choices have a more relevant role. The harmonic passages are dense with cromatisms and the melody is almost entirely built on descending and then ascending minor seventh intervals at the beginning of the first two phrases (*D-E-D* the first time, *C-D-C* the second time). In the first phrase, the melody ends leaning on the sixth and concluding with a descending jump by a major sixth *C-E* the first time ("Just

Fig. 87. Rolling Stones, Lady Jane *(B section).*

Fig. 88. Queen, Bohemian Rhapsody *(extract).*

head this plea, my love"). In the second phrase, instead, from the leaning on the sixth *B* we go down a whole octave to the lower *B* ("On bended knee, my love"). The third and conclusive phrase of the section starts with an ascending jump by a major sixth (*E-C*, "I pledge myself"), which enhances the effect of a romantic courtesan madrigal of the Elizabethan age. Note the correspondence of the sixth with the words "my love". As for our interval, I think I can say that the wide jump by a seventh presents us an open movement, an open hearted expression, maybe a little excessive, though not enough to become sinister as a major seventh, a quite contained expression, as it is apropriate in the halls of the high society. An excessive amplitude that is anyway almost immediately adjusted descending by a semi-tone to the more reassuring and appropriate major sixth.

Finally, an example that is not placed at the beginning of the song and therefore requires a certain knowledge of the tune to be spotted. In *Bohemian Rhapsody* by Queen, we find a melodic phrase built on an meaningful range of a descending minor seventh. In the second phrase of the second verse ("but now I've gone and thrown it all away"), the melody goes up a minor third from *G* to *Bb* and then comes gradually back from *Bb* down a minor seventh to *C*, with a very dramatic effect. A sudden enlargement of the intervals and melodic ranges used up to that point. An expression of rage and frus-tration that foretells the desperation of the whole song.

Semantic field

The seventh interval is a big jump, not a conclusive one, but a re-ally emphatic one, the excessive gesture of someome in the throes of strong emotions: something more than the appropriate measure of a sixth, something less than the definitive octave. In the case of a minor seventh, its dissonant and tense character is slighlty softened, with a melodic tendency to lean on the sixth. Therefore it often proves to be a sentimental expression thrown a little too far and then frequently adjusted to the measure of the interval of the heart. It can also appear affected and contained, only slightly over the top, only slightly over the major sixth. Or it might take a playfully sensual tone, maybe even a caricatural tone.

If we substitute the minor seventh in the *Star Wars* theme, taking the melody immediately to the octave of the second phrase, all the sense of mystery and the melody's narrative arch get lost. Similarly, if we use a major seventh instead of the minor seventh, the effect we get is dramatically different, resulting much more sinister and threatening.

Same thing for the *Watermelon Man*'s melody: should it begin with a descending octave interval, instead of the minor seventh, we would undoubtedly get a more serious and assertive music.

If we try to take the seventh interval away from the second melodic theme in *Lady Jane*, staying on a unison until the major sixth appears, much of the Elizabethan charme of the melody would suddenly disappear.

Harmonic major seventh

The major seventh interval covers a distance of five tones and a half, that is eleven semitones. Just a semitone away from the 'total' interval of an octave. From a harmonic point of view, therefore, it is a dissonant interval with a strong tension towards the tonic note of the scale.

In the construction of the chords as stacking alternating thirds, it is the natural addition to most of the major chords: for example *C-E* (major third), *E-G* (minor third), *G-B* (major third). In this sense, it

Fig. 89. The harmonic major seventh interval G-F#.

can also be perceived as a pleasant added colour to a perfectly consonant triad. On the other hand, when we add it to a minor triad, its dissonant and tense nature is much more evident: for example in an *A minor 7+* chord, *A-C* (minor third), *C-E* (major third), *E-G#* (major third).

The dissonant role of the seventh note in a major scale, called *leading tone*, is a decisive one, though it might result a little hidden, in the most classical and conclusive of the cadence movements, from the chord on the V degree of the scale (dominant chord) to the chord on the I degree (tonic). In the key of *C major*, for instance, the leading tone in the *C major* scale is *B*, just a semitone away from the octave *C*. If we build a triad starting on the fifth note of the scale, we get the *G major* chord: *G-B-D*. Here, *B* plays the temporary role of major third in the *G major* chord. But in the movement towards the tonic *C major* (*C-E-G*) it mantains its leading tone tension that will resolve going up a semitone to the note *C*, tonic note of the tonic chord.

Melodic major seventh

The major seventh is a difficult interval, an extremely wide and yet incomplete interval. There are only a few examples in which the interval is presented in a clear and evident way in the context of a melody. Nonetheless, we can find it in some famous and particularly incisive melodic phrases.

In the theme from the *Superman* soundtrack, written by John Williams, the melody starts with epic jumps by ascending fifths in two phrases that are stretched to a range of a major sixth. And then, here it comes, our ascending major seventh interval *C-C-C-B*, resolving down on the fifth *G* twice, before the real conclusion *B-A-B-C* (higher octave). This major seventh *B* is a long note, falling on the first beat of the measure, that is the strongest beat. Therefore, the jump by a major seventh is located on an important and evident po-

Fig. 90. Superman Theme, *by John Williams.*

sition, it is repeated twice and it is clearly perceived as a deviation from the perfect fifth intervals heard before. We can almost interpret it as the narration of the efforts and attempts needed to come to the fulfillment of the octave.

Take On Me is a song by Norwegian band A-ha that was very famous in the Eighties, thanks to a very innovative videoclip for that time, and also thanks to the display of the singer's vocal abilities: in the chorus, he reached an extension of two octaves and a half. After a melodic start with verses based on small intervals and a rhythmic agitated movement, the chorus immediately starts with a very wide jump by an ascending major seventh, from a low *A* to *G#*, then landing on the higher octave *A* ("Take on me"). The same melodic pattern is then repeated twice, higher and higher, but with a range that is reduced to a sixth: *A-E-F#* the first time (major sixth), *C#-G#-A* the second time (minor sixth). In both cases, the second note of the phrase is used as a foothold just a semitone below the destination note, exactly as the major seventh in the first phrase. The sense conveyed is of a terrific and difficult climb, with a sort of a stumble before achieving the final goal.

The first melodic phrase in the verses in Norah Jones' *Don't Know Why* starts with an ascending jump by a major seventh *Bb-A*, then goes back gradually down to the starting *Bb*, also defining an overall range of a major seventh ("I waited till I saw the sun"). Even when the melodic phrase is repeated without this first note *Bb*, the melodic arch anyway covers a range of a (descending) major seventh. The sense of the interval has been defined, so maintaining the same range is all we need to remain in the same atmosphere. The feeling we get is of something incomplete, something neglected. And the descending movement gives the melody a certain tone of regret.

In *Both Sides Now* by Joni Mitchell, we find a descending major seventh interval *C#-D* in the third melodic phrase of the verse, falling on the words "feather canyons". The amplitude of this jump, con-

Fig. 91. A-ha, Take On Me *(chorus).*

Fig. 92. Norah Jones, Don't Know Why.

trasted by the intimate and step by step movement of the rest of the melody, conveys the image of how deep these canyons are, while the instability of the major seventh also gives us the idea of ephemerality. In the end, the lyrics are describing the clouds, seen as a dream in the past but now perceived as an obstacle for the sun. The major seventh interval fits well the transitory image of clouds and their formations, and also the sense of resignation for what we didn't finish: in the second verse, we find it falling on the line "so many things I would have done".

Semantic field

The major seventh interval is a very wide gesture, yet it does not completely achieve its purpose, a jump that fails the purpose of achieving a goal. A dissonance that sounds unharmonic and unbalanced. A strong emotional expression, yet uncontrolled. Its more natural resolution is on the octave, almost as to adjust a miscalculation, or to make the last effort to get to the goal we aimed at. The major seventh's tension is stronger and more dissonant compared to the minor seventh.

If we take the major seventh away from the *Superman* theme, substituting it with a jump by an octave, the melody loses its epic narrative flow, conveying only a triumphant and pompous sense. In the same way, if we change the major seventh with a minor seventh, the tension to reach the glorious octave becomes much less evident.

Fig. 93. Joni Mitchell, Both Sides Now.

In *Don't Know Why*, we can try to change the overall range of the melody, by shifting the first and last note to create, for instance, an octave, or a sixth interval. In the first case, the melody gets much weaker, since it lacks that fundamental tension. In the latter case, instead, a certain tension remains, but we certainly enter the semantic field related to the interval of the heart, that would colour the song with a completely different meaning and atmosphere.

Chapter 9
The octave

Harmonic octave

The octave interval covers a distance of six tones, that is all the twelve semitones. It is the biggest interval, meaning that the octave is identical to the first note, only in a higher (or lower) register. From a harmonic point of view, it is essentially the same as the unison. It is the essence of consonance. When two voices simultanously play the same note, even if they are separated by an octave, we perceive them as unisons, in a complete absence of motion. The only difference, compared to the unison interval, is that the octave is more open, it conveys a sense of space, generated by the wide distance of twelve semitones separating the two notes.

The octave is the interval of the wide, motionless spaces, and also the interval of identity, of no distance at all, of the perfect totality, of the closing of a circle.

Fig. 94. The harmonic octave interval G-G.

Melodic octave

From a melodic point of view, the octave is a powerful interval, well exemplified by the beginning of the second movement in Beethoven's *Ninth Symphony (opus 125)*, with its three consecutive jumps by a descending octave: *D-D-D / A-A-A / D-D-D*. In the whole phrase, from the first to the last *D*, two whole octaves are covered. It is a majestic, energetic, very exclamatory attack. For each octave, the lower note is repeated, with a rhythmic pattern that frequently returns through all the symphony. In addition, the last conclusive jump by an octave is detached from the previous ones by a whole measure, where the rhythmic pattern is echoed by the timpani, giving even more strength and magnificence to the last fall by an octave.

Fig. 95. Beethoven, Ninth Symphony, opus 125 *(beginning of the second movement).*

The descending octave is also the musical mimic of a shout, a warning, as in Verdi's *Il Trovatore*. In the first scene of the first act, Ferrando enters singing "All'erta! All'erta!" (Watch out! Watch out!) exactly on a descending octave interval with the unison *G-G* that falls down to the lower *G* twice.

The melody in *Singin' in the Rain*, written by Nacho Herb Brown and included in the musical movie by the same name where Gene Kelly sings it, starts with a jump by an octave from *C* to the higher *C*. The second note is longer and falls on the first beat of the measure, the strongest and more accentuated beat. Then the melody gradually

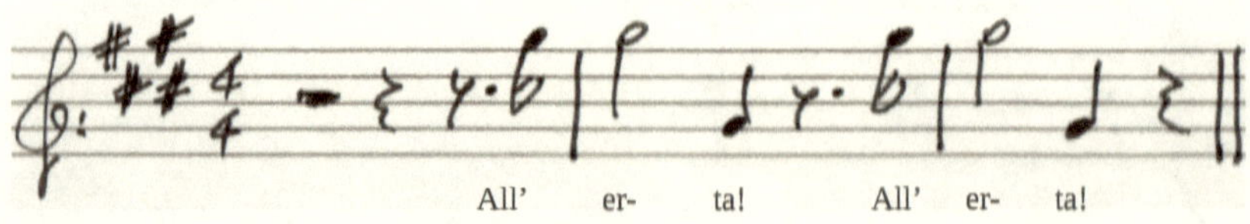

Fig. 96. Verdi, Il Trovatore (All'erta!).

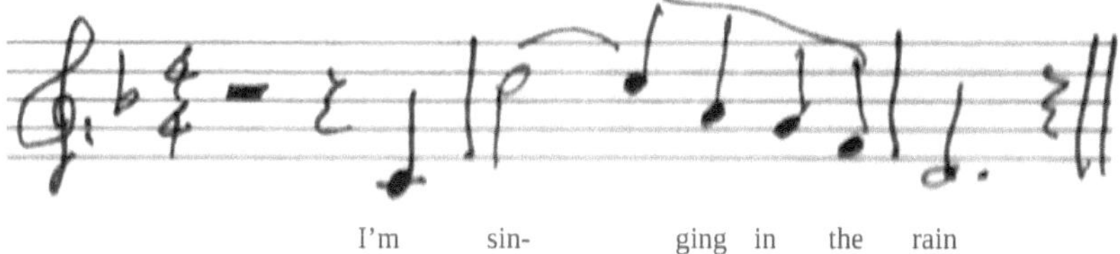

Fig. 97. Singin' in the Rain, *by Nacio Herb Brown.*

goes down to *D*, a tone above the starting note. Here, the feeling is that of a very wide gesture, a jump upwards with your arms open, an explosion of joy.

Also *Over the Rainbow*, that we mentioned earlier in this book, starts with an ascending jump by an octave, from *E* to *E*. This interval on its own gives us an idea of the enormous spaces separating us from that place that is over the rainbow. The sixth, that appears soon after that, tinges the whole atmosphere with a sense of dream and hope. But the octave interval on its own, isolated from the melody and from its sixth, has no melancholic or dreaming colour. It is rather a strong statement, with a gesture that takes off like a rocket.

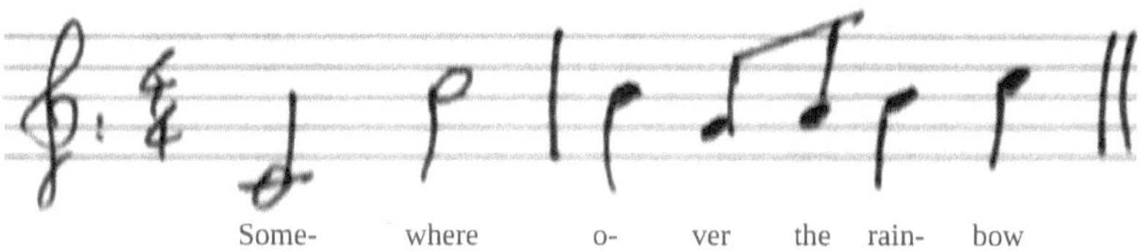

Fig. 98. Over the Rainbow, *by Harold Arlen.*

A last example shows a further possile use of the octave interval. In *Love Me or Leave Me* by Walter Donaldson, interpreted by Ruth Etting in the musical *Whoopee!* in 1928, after an introduction with a

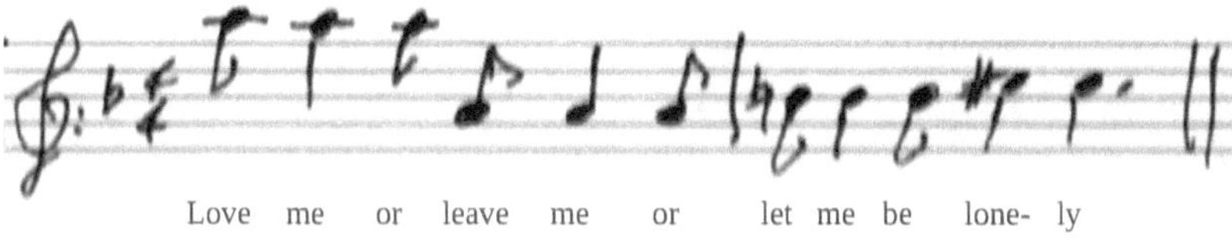

Fig. 99. Love Me or Leave Me, *by Walter Donaldson.*

progressive movement almost as a recitative, the melody starts with a descending jump by an octave from *F* to *F* on the words "Love me or leave me". Here, the separation of these two concepts is sharp and extreme. The octave creates a strong and unbridgeable distance between the two option "love me or leave me".

Semantic field

The enormous distance created by the octave interval indicates enormous spaces and also wide and strong gestures. This interval has a glorious and energetic, imperative tone. When it is descending, it takes the tone of an exclamation that admits no contraddiction, of a warning call, often mimicking the natural voice inflexion when we try to warn someone, for instance, of an impending danger. When it is ascending, it recalls the feeling of a powerful jump, of an opening, even of a rocket's take-off. The lack of tension makes it the interval of decision, confidence, simplicity, stability, identity. Yet, exactly because of these features, it can be used to separate two concepts with an unbridgeable distance. The octave interval highlights the function of the scale degree where it appears: on a tonic, for example, it will sound decisevely afflrmative and conclusive; whereas, if it is placed over a more melodic degree, as the third or the sixth, it will amplify this melodic aspect of the degree.

As an exercise, if we try to substitute the octaves in Beethoven's *Ninth Symphony* with unisons, we can see that the harmonic movement doesn't change very much, but the sense conveyed by those imperious musical exclamations completely disappears.

The gesture on Verdi's "All'erta!" as well would take a completely different sound if, for instance, we sang it on a fourth interval. It is like hearing a suggestion to someone close to you, instead of a shout aiming at distant ears.

Finally, if we try to substitute the starting interval in *Singin' in the Rain* with a sixth, we get a completely different song.

Chapter 10
Extra-large and microtonal intervals

I s there music beyond the octave interval? Is there a semantic field that is smaller than a semitone? The answer to both questions is yes. In our analysis of the intervals and of the ways they have been used to express or convey certain semantic fields, we considered the octave as the totality, the maximum measure possible. In fact – since the eighth note is the same of the first note in the pattern of intervals within a scale – from this note on, the series of intervals repeats itself. Yet, in theory, it is absolutely possible to create wider jumps than an octave, to create 'extra-large' intervals. In the same way, we have considered the semitone as a measuring unit, taking for granted that no smaller distance could exist. In fact, in the Western system based on the equal temperament, there is no smaller distance than a semitone between two notes. Yet acoustic physics allows us to subdivide the distance of a semitone into a great variety of intermediate measurable frequencies: the microtones.

Intervals beyond the octave

Any interval that goes beyond the range of an octave is necessarily a very big, enormous, huge, exaggerated interval, something that goes beyond what is known, beyond what is allowed, a gesture that overflows from the reassuring cup of the octave.

From a harmonic point of view, it is quite frequent that whenever we add notes, that are too close together, to the basic triad of a chord, we opt for a shift to one or two octaves above: for example, adding a second in a triad chord we get the so called ninth chord, since usually that second is raised by an octave, thus changing into a ninth. In these cases, we talk about *compound intervals*: a distance of an eleventh is the sum of a fourth plus an octave. In the poliphonic over-laying of voices or instruments, this stretching of the range without modifying the basic interval often corresponds to an enhanced ener-getic charge: for example, what would happen to an AC/DC's song if the voice sang an octave lower? On the other hand, the general sense of intervals and their consonant or dissonant characteristics don't change when they are shifted a further octave away from the starting note.

From a melodic point of view, instead, we need to take other as-pects into consideration. The range of an octave is a comfortable range to sing, for any voice. Beyond this limit, things get more com-plicated. Consequently, it will be difficult to find vocal lines with jumps that go beyond the octave. For the instruments, things are dif-ferent. In this case, the exaggerated interval that goes beyond the oc-tave is often perceived as an absurdity, something alien, a non human amplitude. The more we get far from the octave, the more the disso-nant intervals are difficult to decode; accordingly, our ear perceives them more in this light of an exaggerating and other-than-human sense, while the consonant intervals are more easily decoded and align with their equivalents within the octave.

An example of a jump by an ascending minor (or flat) ninth is at the beginning of *Killing in the Name* by Rage Against the Machine. Here the bass, all alone, plays three low *D*s and then three *Eb*s an octave above. This line is definitely prominent, since there is no har-mony or melody that goes with it, and it is built only on this interval. The range is exaggerated, though it is just a little beyond the octave, and the effect is alienating. Should we play the same *Eb* an octave lower, just a minor second from the starting note, the tension would be very different, though the interval in itself has not really changed.

Fig. 100. The bassline at the beginning of Killing in the Name, *by Rage Against the Machine.*

Microtonality

Any distance between two notes that is smaller than a semitone falls into the category of the so called *microtonal intervals*. Western art music practice always relied mainly on a division of the octave in distances that were no smaller than a semitone. Even more so with the advent of the equal temperament. This is true at least until the beginning of the 20th century. In several musical traditions, developed on a different division of the octave, we often find notes that, at least to our ear, sound similar to the notes we get when we use microtonal intervals. This is particularly evident in many Eastern and Middle Eastern musical cultures (Turkish, Arab and so on). Yet similar intervals do exist also in many folk traditions that are still alive in the Western world. Without venturing into a study of a thousand different folk European and American traditions, just think of the blues, which had a great success, taking roots as a worldwide accepted musical language. One of blues main features is the *blue note*, a note that is halfway, usually between the minor third and the major third. Since it was difficult to perform it on instruments based on the equal temperament, this note originated what is usually defined as a *neutral third*, built with the simultaneous presence of the minor and major thirds in the scale (and sometimes in the typical 'rubato' chord arpeggios), with an effect that simulate an intermediate note.

Many 20th century's composers experimented with the possibilities of scales that were expanded to include microtonal intervals. These scales are often made of 24 notes within the range of an octave. To obtain this effect with instruments that are not suited to produce all the necessary notes, they used several strategies, such as the co-presence of two pianos playing together but tuned on a different reference tone, with a difference smaller than a semitone between them, so that one piano could play the notes that the other piano couldn't. On string instruments, it is possible to get microtonal intervals with the bending technique: pulling the string upwards (or downwards) we can alter the intonation without getting to the next semitone. This technique is very popular on blues guitar. In *Are You Gonna Be My Girl* by Jet, we find at the beginning an isolated bass riff, then taken up in the song also in unison with the guitar. Here, on the higher note of the riff, we clearly hear a longer *D* compared

Fig. 101. The bassline at the beginning of Are You Gonna Be My Girl, *by Jet.*

to the other notes, which is altered through a bending to a pitch that is more or less halfway between *D* and *D#*.

On the other hand, some instruments have no fixed intonation: for instance all the wind instruments. We can find an example of microtonal intervals in the clarinet's glissando at the beginning of George Gershwin's *Rhapsody in Blue*. In the passage from a low *F* to the *Bb* two octaves higher, the sound slips through the whole frequency spectrum, including microtones. This same effect can also be created with an electronic instrument, like a synthesizer or a theremin, for example. When used in an ascending manner, typically on an amplitude of one or more octaves, it is called a *riser*: in modern pop music there are many examples of *risers* created with electronic instruments. Yet this effect was already extensively used in many earlier psychedelic and electronic songs. We find examples in *One of These Days or Set Controls for the Heart of the Sun* by Pink Floyd, in *Master of the Universe* by Hawkwind and in many songs by Ozric Tentacles or Gong. In the case of Gong, rather than a *riser*, it is often an expressive glissando (usually performed with special guitar techniques or on wind instruments, specifically the doudouk, an Armenian instrument played by Didier Malherbe). In *Oxygene* by Jean-Michel Jarre we find an effect that mimics the sound of the wind, realised with a synthesizer that moves around microtonal intervals. In all these glissando examples, it is difficult to clearly iden-

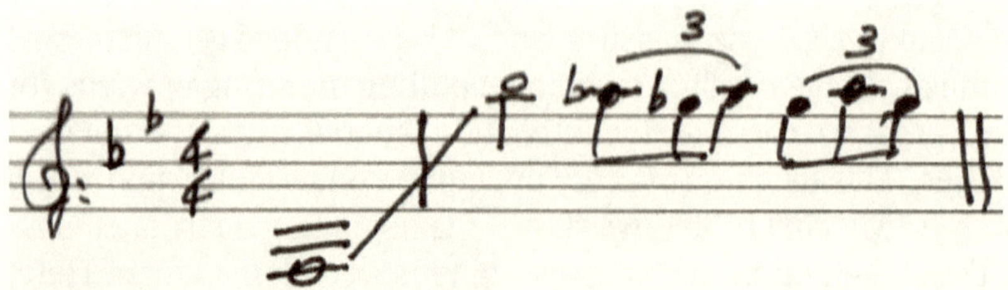

Fig. 102. George Gershwin, Rhapsody in Blue.

tify the single passing notes, since the movement is quite fast and our ear is more focused on defining the starting point, the arriving point and the range of the journey. We find ascending movements somehow similar to *risers* also in David Bowie's *Space Oddity* and in Elton John's *Rocket Man*. In both cases they are associated with the idea of a space rocket taking off. In both cases, though, it is the electric guitar that creates this effect: it is difficult to say if they are really microtonal passages, but the basic principle is the same. In 2017, King Gizzard and the Lizard Wizard published an album called *Flying Microtonal Banana*. In this album, many scales are created by substituting 'normal' intervals with microtonal intervals. To get this effect, they even modified a guitar, by placing the frets following a non uniform pattern, so that it could play some microtonal intervals instead of the usual semitones. David Bennett made a very clear and instructive video on microtones: *Microtonality in Western Music* (www.youtube.com/watch?v=q1XOnIk2ai8).

The voice is anyway the best instrument to sing microtones. In blues, we find many examples, especially clear in Bessie Smith's vocal melodies, for instance. David Bennet himself has been quoted earlier, talking about the descending major second interval in *Yesterday*: there he spotted a vocal intonation that very much recalled a microtonal interval. Similar vocal intonations can be found in many other examples. In *Whole Lotta Rosie* by AC/DC, the voice starts with a line all developed on the repetition of an *A*, that ends leaning on the ascending minor third *C* ("Wanna tell you a story"). But the way the melody is performed conveys the idea of a progressive ascent, of rising tension. There is no semitone passage, but there are microtones, creating the sense of rising and energy that otherwise that melodic phrase would not have.

To conclude this book, I hope that all this dissertation and the examples suggested have awakened your curiosity to study and experiment, rather than providing a sterile knowledge of the musical intervals. Wether you are musicians or simple enthusiasts about music, I hope I managed to contribute a little to a greater basic musical competence. So I exhort you to read the other books as well from this small series. In *From Intervals to Melody* I will get further deeper on the subjects regarding the intervals, with some examples analysed within their melodic context. Moreover, I wil try to lay the foundations for a study of melody as a founding element of music, something that unluckily the musical theory landscape still lacks. Finally, *Musical Structures* will deal with the subject of the form of the songs, from a historical and evolutive point of view and from a formal and semantic perspective. The musical structure as a strategy for narration. Up to the musical forms that try to destroy the structure.

Whatever your approach to music is, as enthusiasts or professionals, as theorists or musicians, please remember the rules that I believe are the golden rules of musical analysis. The first and fundamental one is that theory always comes after practice: first someone does something, then someone else talks about it. Any theory that tries to be prescribing instead of describing is dangerous. The second rule is that music, in its essence, is relation. Although it might be useful to isolate its constitutive elements to observe them from a closer point of view and understand their mechanisms, no musical analysis should ever forget the context: the other musical elements, the historical and social period, the genre, the place where the music is performed and so on.

Enjoy the music!

About the author

Roberto Cruciani is a musicologist and musician. Born in 1972, he studied Musicology in the Nineties at the University of Bologna. In 2005, he wrote the book *Scrivere Canzoni* (How to Write Songs, published by Dino Audino Editore). In 2010 he wrote the book *Costruire una melodia* (How to Build a Melody), again published by Dino Audino Editore. In 2016 he held a series of six meetings called *Bass Talks*, on the role of the electric bass in the shaping of musical structures, on the importance of knowing and recognising musical intervals, and on the strategies to arrange a cover that include a change on the level of musical structure. Between 2020 and 2022, he participated as a speaker to some of the conferences in the context of the project *Il cervello e le sue meraviglie* (Brain and its Wonders), organised in Rome by Abraxa Teatro, on the relationship between neuroscience and arts. As a musician, he is the bass player of the blues-rock band Fleurs du Mal, for which he recorded in several Lps and played in many national and international tours. The latest Fleurs du Mal's Lp also sees the participation of the New Orleans harmonicist Andy J Forest. He's been also founder and bass player in several other bands, including Grey Lagoon, which gave him the opportunity to work with Daevid Allen (Gong, Soft Machine) and Niels Van Hoorn (Strange Attractor, Legendary Pink Dots). Between 2003 and 2004 he was also the bass player for the songwriter Flavio Giurato. At the end of the Nineties he also participated as a musician in an international experimental theatre group based in Malta, Groups For Human Encounter.

Music Talks

The series *Music Talks* is made of three small books on musical theory, and offers an approach to musical analysis where practice is on the foreground, based on the assumption that theory should only explain practice, rather than dictating its rules. Each book of the series is rich with analysis and practical examples, using songs that are usually excluded from the books on musical theory. The main focus is on the ear, on the listening and on the construction of melody as a central element in the musical experience, too often confined in the background by the mainstream musical theory. In the appendix of the last two books, a number of exercises will allow the reader to test his or her skills in the musical analysis, using the tools provided in the books.

In the series *Music Talks*:

1 – The Intervals
2 – From Intervals to Melody
3 – Musical Structures

All these books are also available in Italian.